10.28.97
gift

The
Vegetarian
NO-CHOLESTEROL
Family-Style
Cookbook

Also by Kate Schumann and Virginia Messina, M.P.H., R.D.

The Vegetarian No-Cholesterol Barbecue Cookbook
(St. Martin's Press, 1994)

The
Vegetarian
NO-CHOLESTEROL
Family-Style
Cookbook

by Kate Schumann and
Virginia Messina, M.P.H., R.D.

St. Martin's Griffin ❧ New York

Production Editor: David Stanford Burr

Library of Congress Cataloging-in-Publication Data

Schumann, Kate.
        The vegetarian no-cholesterol family-style cookbook / Kate
    Schumann and Virginia Messina.—1st ed.
            p. cm.
        ISBN 0-312-13612-9
        1. Vegetarian cookery.   2. Low-cholesterol diet—
Recipes. I. Messina, Virginia.   II. Title.
        TX837.S323   1995
        641.5'636—dc20   95-24048
                                                           CIP

First St. Martin's Griffin Edition: October 1995

10 9 8 7 6 5 4 3 2 1

*To our mothers, Willie Kisch and Harriett Penney, who taught us
not only the basics of cooking but also the joys.*

Contents

Acknowledgments

One of the special features of this book is that it includes favorite family recipes from so many wonderful cooks. This book would never have been written without their help and we are grateful to everyone who contributed so generously to this endeavor: Steve Altshuld, Linda Arcadia, chef Jay Brinkley, Mary Clifford, Ruth Cornelius, Claude Demick, Suzanne Essick, John Futhey, Rose Geiger, Marjorie Groff, John Hilton, Leonard Karlin, Mary Kayaselcuk, Melanie and Oliver King-Smith, Polly Knappen, Valerie Parker, Lorna Sass, Cherie Soria, Debra Wasserman, the folks at the Texas Society for Animal Rights.

Dr. Neal Barnard, president of the Physicians Committee for Responsible Medicine, provided the spark that led to this book when he set out to compile favorite recipes for healthy holiday feasting. We're grateful for his ideas, his enthusiasm, and for giving us the opportunity to share this recipe collection with readers.

As always, our agent Patti Breitman earns our warmest thanks for her support, her enthusiasm, and her guidance.

We thank Jennifer Weis and Tina Lee at St. Martin's Press who so cheerfully and skillfully guided this book through its miraculous evolution from scribbled, flour-dusted recipes to a real cook-book.

Finally, we thank our husbands, Mark Messina and Ned Schumann, those indefatigable taste testers for their help, support, and patience.

Acknowledgments

The Vegetarian
NO-CHOLESTEROL
Family-Style
Cookbook

Introduction

For most of us, food, more than anything else, brings back memories of family gatherings, traditional holiday celebrations, and the comforts of home. Sometimes we long for those old-fashioned "comfort foods"—the savory, warming stews that graced the family dinner tables of our childhood and the gingerbread that tasted and smelled like Grandma's kitchen. But with the trend toward low-fat cooking, are these favorite traditional recipes—most of which are loaded with fat and cholesterol—destined to become nothing more than fond memories? Happily, the answer is no.

You can still enjoy traditional eating experiences—but without all that fat and cholesterol. We've re-created a variety of old family recipes that for us, and for others who contributed to this book, bring back the warmest and happiest memories. Some of the recipes are such close cousins to those you might remember from your own childhood kitchen, that it is hard to tell them apart. For others, we've added new taste twists to old-fashioned recipes. Instead of buttermilk pancakes or French toast, try our wonderful spiced pumpkin pancakes or banana French toast. Chili is such a family favorite that we've offered it in a variety of ways—as a traditional recipe served over rice, as a spicy

1

chili soup, and as easy, savory chili barbecued beans. If you long for homemade burritos, we think you'll love our version made with black beans. And for birthdays and other special occasions, you'll find rich chocolate cake, spicy carrot cake, chocolaty brownies, and real old-fashioned favorites like rice pudding.

Family-style eating includes not only all those down-home basics, but also more festive dishes for holidays and other special occasions. We've suggested new, healthier menus to help you plan feasts for Thanksgiving, Christmas, Hanukkah, Kwanzaa, and other festive occasions. We've included winning recipes from the "Healthy Holiday Recipe Contest" sponsored by the Physicians Committee for Responsible Medicine to come up with menus that are truly special.

The secret to preparing all these healthy, satisfying dishes is knowing the appropriate substitutions for fatty, cholesterol-laden ingredients. You'll find low-fat cooking to be a snap when you discover some simple ways to substitute for the meat, eggs, and dairy products in your favorite recipes. In most cases, you can do so with familiar ingredients that you already have in your kitchen. In others, we'll introduce you to some ingredients that may be new to you, and that will make your cooking more interesting and fun.

This is a collection of recipes for those who love to eat and who warm to all the memories that family-style cooking conjures up.

CHAPTER ONE

A Healthy Menu

Healthy eating is a simpler concept than you might imagine. It can be summed up in one sentence. Plan meals around whole plant foods: grains, vegetables, fruits, and legumes. When people eat this way, they have much lower rates of heart disease, cancer, diabetes, and other chronic diseases.

It's easy to see why such diets promote good health. They tend to be low in fat, since plant foods are generally much lower in fat than animal foods. They are lower in cholesterol, which is found only in animal foods. Plant-based diets are also much higher in health-promoting fiber, which is found only in plant foods. Finally, plant foods are rich in compounds called *phytochemicals*. These are not nutrients, but are chemicals that have powerful disease-fighting properties. Phytochemicals are probably the main reason that people who eat diets rich in fruits and vegetables have much lower rates of cancer. Fruits and vegetables are especially rich in phytochemicals, but all plant foods contain them. Animal foods don't have any phytochemicals.

For the healthiest menu, make grains the backbone of your diet. Some people are stymied by the idea of grain-based meals. But many family favorites, like spaghetti, chili over rice, or sloppy joes served on rolls, actually make generous use of grains.

These foods are rich in fiber—particularly the type of fiber that protects against colon disease—starch, protein, B vitamins, iron, and other minerals. Processed grains are less nutritious than whole grains, but they are still nutrient-rich foods. Do try to use whole grains as much as possible, but it is fine to include some processed grains in your diet as well.

To make grains the center of your diet, plan all your meals around these foods. Build breakfasts around toasted whole grain breads, hearty hot cereals like 7-grain cereal or oatmeal, or for a fast breakfast, ready-to-eat cereals. Old-fashioned favorites like bran flakes or shredded wheat are among the healthiest choices. You might also start the day with baked goods like pancakes, whole grain muffins, or French toast.

For lunch, try the all-American favorite—a sandwich. You might explore whole grain breads other than whole wheat. Wonderful choices include granola bread, oat bread, and multigrain breads. Other good lunch ideas include pasta or rice salads with chopped vegetables and reduced-fat dressing. Or carry a thermos to work filled with hearty, hot soups like mushroom barley.

Most of us were raised to think first of meat when planning a dinner menu. But a healthier approach is to fill the dinner plate with a mountain of fluffy, seasoned brown rice, wheat berries, quinoa, or any of your favorite grains. Top this with steamed or sautéed vegetables or with a savory sauce of beans. You'll notice that most of the entrées in this book make generous use of grains, so they will automatically help you to make these foods the center of your diet.

Explore the wonderful selection of grains and grain products in the supermarket, natural foods store, and in international markets. Don't shy away from trying some of the newer ones just because you've never cooked them before. Keep it simple by seasoning hot grains with fresh herbs or with your favorite spices. Or just toss them with fresh garlic, onion, and grated ginger root.

It's easy to make your snacks grain-based as well. When you feel like munching on something, choose bagels, graham crackers, muffins, or popcorn.

• VEGETABLES AND FRUITS •

Unfortunately the average American eats just two or three servings each day of vegetables and fruits combined. The National Cancer Institutes suggests at least five servings a day and we think it is a good idea to eat even more than that. People who consume generous amounts of fruits and vegetables have much lower risks of cancer. Fruits are protective against cancer, but not to nearly the extent that vegetables are. So eat plenty of fruits, but be extra generous in your consumption of vegetables. Since a serving is just ½ cup cooked or 1 cup raw vegetables, this isn't at all difficult. Add vegetables to soups and stews. Snack on raw vegetables throughout the day. Have a salad with your lunch and then a couple of servings of cooked vegetables at dinner.

Take a new look at the fruits and vegetables in the produce department of your local grocery store. Chances are there are many things there that you have never tasted before. You'll be in for some pleasant surprises as you explore the vast selection of these foods.

When you visit the produce section of the store, buy what is in season. In-season fruits and vegetables are most economical, have the freshest taste, and the best nutritional profile. Then, get the most out of your vegetables—both taste and nutrient-wise—by gently steaming them or sautéing in a broth or a tiny bit of olive oil. For the best flavor, don't cook vegetables until they are mush. Rather cook them until they are just tender and heated through.

• LEGUMES •

Happily, many good cooks are rediscovering legumes. These are beans, peas, and lentils. For years, beans turned up on American tables as an occasional side dish of baked beans or as one ingredient in soup. But these foods have a rich history in American cooking that

---

A Healthy Menu   7

is finally being rediscovered. Baked beans are one of the true American originals. Native Americans taught the first English settlers to bake beans flavored with onions, molasses, and bacon in pits in the ground. Baked beans continue to be a New England favorite and it seems as though there are as many Boston baked bean recipes as there are Bostonians.

Southern cuisine makes good use of black-eyed peas, a bean brought to this country by African slaves. In the Southwest, pinto and black beans play a starring role in many dishes with a south-of-the-border flair that is so common to the cooking of that region.

The return of the bean to American tables is good news, since this food is a powerhouse of nutrition. Most beans are very low in fat and all are chock-full of protein, B vitamins, iron, calcium, and other minerals. They are also rich in the type of fiber that helps to lower blood cholesterol levels and control blood glucose levels. We've included a number of bean dishes from different parts of the country; any are perfect as a main dish for dinner or lunch. We've also included a couple of bean spreads that make good sandwich stuffers.

The soybean represents a special category of the legume group since it gives rise to a number of products that are perfect for replacing meat and dairy in your menus. Foods made from soybeans include tofu, tempeh, soy milk, and miso (see the following chapter for descriptions of these foods). Since soybeans are quite a bit higher in fat than other legumes, many soy foods contain a fair amount of fat. However, they are usually lower in fat than the meat or dairy they replace; also, like other plant foods, soy foods are cholesterol-free and are low in saturated fat. A number of reduced-fat versions of tofu and soy milk are now available.

• NUTS AND SEEDS •

Nuts and seeds are rich in fiber, protein, calcium, and minerals. However, they are also very high in fat. They can add wonderful flavor and texture to dishes and we include them in many of our recipes. A serving or two of these foods, in a diet that is generally low in fat is fine. But don't overdo it. Add a few tablespoons to your recipes but don't snack on handfuls of these foods.

Fats and oils often play a big role in traditional family-style recipes. In the next chapter, we'll show you how to minimize these foods in your cooking. Although you need a little fat in your diet, this requirement for fat is quite small. Most people get plenty from the small amounts that are present in most plant foods. Those who eat meat and dairy products generally get too much. So there is absolutely no requirement for added fats in your meals. That doesn't mean that you can never have them. It's the total amount of fat in your diet that matters; if your diet is generally low in fat, then a few added servings of fats is fine.

It's easy to plan healthy, low-fat, cholesterol-free meals without much attention to detail. First, for all meals, fill your plate with whole grains—in the form of rice or other grains, cereals, and breads. Make sure each meal includes several generous servings of vegetables and or fruits. Serve legumes frequently—either by themselves or as an ingredient in soups, stews, or salads. These are the foods that are necessities in the diet.

The superior health of vegetarians throughout the world is a testament to the fact that there is no need for meat in the diet. In fact, the less meat you eat, the better off you are. Dairy foods are not needed in the diet either. In many parts of the world, people enjoy superior bone health even though dairy foods are uncommon in their diets.

Your best bet for healthy eating is to focus on those foods that are dietary essentials—grains, fruits, vegetables, and legumes—and to minimize added fats and animal products. Small servings of nuts or seeds and vegetables oils are fine for occasional use. They can also help children to meet calorie and nutrient needs.

In addition to being low in fat and rich in fiber, plant-based menus are also rich in nutrients. You might give some attention to a few nutrients in particular. For children, especially, you'll want to be certain you are including several good sources of calcium in the diet every day. And, since vitamin B12 isn't found in any plant foods, be sure to use foods that are fortified with this nutrient (Red Star brand nutritional yeast, number T6635, is a good source and many cereals are also fortified) or use a supplement.

· PLANT SOURCES OF CALCIUM ·

Legumes (1 cup cooked)   *milligrams of calcium*

Chick-peas	78
Great Northern beans	121
Kidney beans	50
Lentils	37
Lima beans	52
Navy beans	128
Pinto beans	82
Black beans	103
Vegetarian baked beans	128

Soy Foods

Soybeans, 1 cup cooked	175
Tofu, ½ cup	120 to 350
Tempeh, ½ cup	77
TVP, ½ cup rehydrated	85
Soy milk, 1 cup	84
Soy milk, fortified, 1 cup	250–300
Soy nuts	252

Nuts and Seeds (2 tablespoons)

Almonds	50
Almond butter	86
Brazil nuts	50
Sesame seeds	176
Tahini	128

Vegetables (½ cup cooked)

Bok choy	79
Broccoli	89
Collard greens	178
Kale	90
Mustard greens	75
Butternut squash	42

Sweet potato	35
Turnip greens	125

Fruits

Dried figs, 5	258
Orange	56
Raisin, ⅔ cup	53
Calcium-fortified orange juice	300

Grains

Corn bread (2-ounce piece)	133
Corn tortilla	53
English muffin	92
Pita bread (1 small pocket)	31

Other Foods

Blackstrap Molasses, 1 tablespoon	187
Rice Dream, fortified, 1 cup	240
Vegelicious, 1 cup	240
Take Care, 1 cup	240

· HOW TO COOK GRAINS ·

There is a wonderful selection of grains available to cooks. Some are old-fashioned favorites like cornmeal, barley, and oats. Others, such as quinoa, spelt, kamut, and amaranth, are new to many but have actually been around for centuries.

The technique for cooking most grains is basically the same, although the amount of water you use and the cooking time varies.

1. Rinse the grain thoroughly.
2. Pretoast the grains. This step is optional. In many cases it makes the grain cook more evenly and enhances the flavor. But because one of the virtues of grains is that they are so

easy to prepare, this optional step may seem like too much trouble. If so, feel free to skip it. If you want to toast your grains, just heat a large heavy skillet, add the rinsed grain, and stir it until the water has evaporated. Continue stirring until the grains begin to pop.

3. Measure liquid (usually water or vegetable broth) into a heavy pot with a tight-fitting lid and bring the water to a boil. (Grains will not cook well in tomato sauce, so add any tomato products after cooking is completed.)

4. Add the grain, return to a boil, then lower to simmer. Place lid on and cook until all the water is absorbed.

5. Most grains will cook best if you add salt after cooking is completed.

· COOKING TIMES FOR GRAINS ·

Amounts are for 1 cup dry, uncooked grain

Grain	Cups liquid	Cooking time	Yield in cups
Amaranth	2½	20–25 minutes	3
Barley (hulled)	3	1½ hours	3½–4
Barley (pearl)	3	50 minutes	3½
Bulgur	2	20 minutes	3
Couscous	2	5 minutes	3
Kamut	3	2 hours	2¾
Millet	2	25 minutes	3
Quinoa	2	15 minutes	3
Spelt	3	2 hours	3
Triticale	3	2 hours	2½
Wheat berries	3	2 hours	3

PRESSURE COOKING GRAINS

Because some whole grains take a long time to cook, we recommend using a pressure cooker. The cooking procedure is exactly the same, but the time needed to cook the grain is much less. In some cases you will use less water, too. When cooking barley, buckwheat, kamut, and oats in the pressure cooker, add several teaspoons of oil to control foaming.

• GRAIN COOKING TIMES FOR PRESSURE COOKER •

Instructions are for cooking 1 cup dried, uncooked grain

Grain	Cups of liquid	Minutes under high pressure	Yield in cups
Amaranth	1¾	4	2
Barley (hulled)	3	40	3½
Barley (pearl)	3	18	3½
Buckwheat	1¾	3	2
Bulgur	1½	6	3
Kamut	3	40–45	2½
Millet	2–2½	12	3½
Spelt	3	40–45	2½
Triticale	3	35–45	2
Wheat berries	3	35–45	2

• HOW TO COOK BEANS •

The first step in preparing dried beans is to rinse them thoroughly. Then, to greatly reduce cooking time, most beans (the exceptions are lentils, split peas, and black-eyed peas) should be soaked for several hours. Smaller beans require only about 4 hours soaking time; larger ones should be soaked for 8 hours or overnight. Use any of the following soaking methods.

SOAKING METHOD 1

1. Place the beans in a large bowl or pot and add 2 cups fresh cold water for each cup of dried beans.

A Healthy Menu

2. Place in the refrigerator and allow to soak for 4 to 8 hours.
3. Drain the beans thoroughly.

SOAKING METHOD 2

If you suffer from gas when you eat beans, try this soaking technique:

1. Place the rinsed beans in a large pot with 3 cups of water for each cup of dried beans. Bring to a boil and boil for 2 minutes. Drain the beans.
2. Add fresh water, again using 3 cups water for each cup of beans. Let soak for 6 or more hours in the refrigerator.
3. Drain the beans and cook according to the following directions.

SOAKING METHOD 3: THE QUICK-SOAK METHOD

If you forget to soak your beans, try this quick-soak method.

1. Cover the beans with water and bring to a boil.
2. Remove from the heat, cover the pot, and let stand at room temperature for 1 hour.

COOKING DRIED BEANS

Be sure to drain the beans well after you have soaked them. Then place in a large heavy pot with 3 cups water for each cup of soaked beans, or 4 cups water for each cup unsoaked beans.

Bring the water to a boil. Reduce the heat, cover the pot, and simmer until the beans are tender. Use the cooking chart opposite to approximate cooking times for different varieties of beans.

• Cooking Times for Beans •

Yields are for 1 cup of dried, uncooked beans.

Beans	Cooking Time in Hours Soaked	Unsoaked	Yield in Cups
Anasazi	2	2½–3	2
Aduki	1–1½	2–3	2
Black	1½–2	2–3	2
Black-eyed peas	½	1	2
Cannellini	1–1½	2	2
Chickpeas	2	3½–4	2½
Cranberry	2	2–3	2½
Great Northern	1–1½	2–3	2¼
Kidney	1½–2	2–3	2
Lentils*		½–¾	2
Lima	¾–1	1½	2
Navy	1½–2	2½–3	2
Pinto	1½–2	2–3	2
Soybeans	2–3	3–4	2½
Split peas*		¾	2

*Lentils and split peas don't need to be soaked before cooking.

PRESSURE COOKING BEANS

1. Use 3 cups of water for each cup soaked beans, or 4 cups water for each cup unsoaked beans.
2. If you are using a jiggle-top pressure cooker, add 1 tablespoon oil for each cup dried beans.
3. Lock the lid into place and bring to high pressure.
4. Cook at high pressure for time indicated on the following chart.
5. Release the pressure quickly, according to the directions for your cooker.
6. Test the beans and return to high pressure for a few minutes if they aren't quite done.

· COOKING TIMES FOR BEANS IN A PRESSURE COOKER ·

Instructions are for 1 cup dried, uncooked beans.

Beans	Minutes Under High Pressure Soaked	Unsoaked	Yield in Cups
Aduki	5–9	14–20	2
Anasazi	4–7	20–22	2
Black	9–11	20–25	2
Black-eyed peas*		9–11	2
Cannellini	9–12	22–25	2
Chickpeas	10–12	30–40	2½
Cranberry	9–12	30–35	2¼
Great Northern	8–12	25–30	2¼
Kidney	10–12	20–25	2
Lentils*		7–10	2
Limas	5–7	12–15	2½
Navy	6–8	15–25	2
Pinto	4–6	22–25	2¼
Soybeans	9–12	25–35	2¼
Split peas*		8–10	2

*Black-eyed peas, lentils, and split peas do not need to be soaked before cooking.

The Vegetarian No-Cholesterol Family-Style Cookbook

CHAPTER TWO

Ingredients for Healthy Family-Style Cooking

A critical issue in healthy eating is keeping fat intake on the low side; we would suggest no more than 15 to 20 percent of your calories. But instead of indulging in laborious calculations or examining the fat content of every recipe you eat, consider the following:

Minimize or omit the animal products in your diet. These are the biggest contributors of fat to your meals and the *only* contributor of cholesterol. (Cholesterol is never found in plant foods.)

Limit your use of processed convenience foods. We know that some of these items just make life plain easier. You'll notice that we are not opposed to using the quickest approach to meal planning; some of our recipes call for canned beans and we've even recommended a few quick mixes to help you put dinner on the table fast. But keep in mind that most convenience foods pile on the fat.

Defat your recipes wherever possible, using some of these hints:

- Prepare vegetables without added fats and serve with herbs, a squeeze of fresh lemon juice, or nonfat salad dressing. With the exception of avocados and olives, vegetables are almost fat-free.

- When using vegetable oil in cooking, be sure to measure it. One teaspoon of oil may be a tiny amount, but it contains 45 calories and 5 grams of fat.
- Reduce your use of fatty spreads like margarine, butter, peanut butter, and mayonnaise. Try some of the following instead:

Bean spreads. Mash cooked beans with chopped onions and celery, herbs or spices, and your favorite condiments such as lemon juice, salsa, mustard, or ketchup to create your own tasty spreads for sandwiches.

Fruit spreads.

Low-fat tofu blended with herbs and lemon juice.

- You can reduce the fat in nearly any cake or cookie recipe by at least a quarter and sometimes much more. Baking with whole wheat pastry flour or with unbleached white flour will help to keep low-fat baked goods more tender. You can also replace some of the fat with puréed moist ingredients like mashed bananas, blended tofu, or puréed prunes.
- Use nonfat dressings on salads
- For dishes that call for onions or other ingredients to be sautéed in oil, try sautéing in sherry or dry wine instead. Vegetable broth, tomato juice, and even apple juice are other good choices.
- Perk up the flavors in your low-fat dishes by using fresh herbs, sun-dried tomatoes (not the kind packed in oil), fresh ginger, or freshly squeezed lemon or lime juice.
- Try a few drops of black walnut extract in rice dishes instead of nuts.
- Use blended tofu in dishes that call for cream.
- Thicken soups and stews with puréed vegetables or mashed potatoes.
- Low-fat tofu blended with cooked vegetables makes a rich sauce to serve over rice or pasta.
- Use nonfat cooking methods. That means baking, steaming, or simmering foods whenever possible.

- Invest in a few nonstick pots and pans so that you don't need to add fat to keep foods from sticking.
- Braise foods instead of sautéing them in oil. Cook onions, garlic, and other vegetables in a small amount of vegetable stock, wine, or sherry.
- Season vegetables with herb-flavored vinegar or melt a tiny bit of margarine with some Dijon mustard and a few squeezes of fresh lemon juice.
- Try one of the new fat substitutes designed for baking. These are a combination of puréed dried fruits and they can substitute for as much as half the fat in cookies, cakes, and muffins. Two good choices are Just Like Shortenin' and WonderSlim, both available in natural food stores.

· EGG SUBSTITUTES ·

Eggs bind ingredients together in recipes. In baked goods, they also make products lighter and fuller by helping to leaven them. In the process, they add fat and cholesterol to recipes. For cholesterol-free cooking, try some of the following egg replacers.

IN BAKED GOODS

- Flax Seed. This is one of the best egg replacers we know for baked products. Grind 3 level tablespoons of flax seed in a blender until it is a very fine powder. Then add ½ cup cold water and blend until the mixture is frothy and viscous. It should have the same texture as well-beaten whole eggs and is equal to about 2 large eggs. Add the mixture to your batter when it calls for eggs. You can refrigerate the mixture for several days.
- Soy flour. This is another excellent egg substitute for baking. For each egg in a recipe, substitute 1 heaping tablespoon of soy flour and 1 tablespoon of water. This works well in cakes, muffins, or cookies that call for up to 3 eggs.
- In some products that don't require a great deal of leavening and that call for only 1 egg, such as pancakes, it is usually fine

to leave the egg out. Be sure to add 2 or 3 additional tablespoons of liquid to the batter.

- Mashed fruits. The addition of mashed banana or applesauce or puréed prunes can replace the moisture of an egg and make a product somewhat tender. Use ¼ cup mashed banana, applesauce, or puréed prunes to replace 1 egg. Of course, this will change the flavor of your product. It will also give you a slightly heavier baked good since the fruit doesn't leaven the product. When using fruit to replace the egg in baked goods, try adding an extra ½ teaspoon of baking powder for each egg omitted from the recipe.
- Try this mixture to replace 1 egg in baked goods: 2 tablespoons white flour, ½ tablespoon vegetable oil, 2 tablespoons water, ½ teaspoon baking powder. Mix them together and add to the batter where an egg is called for.
- Commercial egg replacer is also available. This is a powdered mixture of potato starch, tapioca flour, and leavening agents. We've used it with varying degrees of success. In some baked products, the end result is fairly dry, but in others it works pretty well. You'll need to experiment a bit to find out where it works best for you.

In vegetarian cooking, you might find that you need something to help hold together the ingredients in a veggie burger mixture or in a bean and grain loaf. Try one of the following:

- Tomato paste. Thin it just a bit with water but not too much or it will lose its capacity to hold the recipe together.
- Tahini. Try mixing tahini with a little bit of tomato paste for a nice flavor and some good binding quality.
- Blended tofu. For an excellent binder, purée 4 ounces soft tofu with 1 to 2 tablespoons white flour.
- Mashed potatoes.
- Flour, matzo meal, or quick oats. Use these sparingly since they can give your burger or loaf a heavy, dense quality.
- Moistened bread crumbs.

· REPLACING DAIRY PRODUCTS IN COOKING ·

One of the easiest ways to reduce cholesterol and saturated fat in your diet is to replace dairy products with vegetable alternatives. Nondairy milks can do just about anything that cow's milk can do in cooking. Try them in puddings, cakes, cream sauces, soups, or over morning cereal. Soy milks are the most popular choice, but there are also wonderful milks made from almonds or rice.

Tofu is a great cheese imitator. Soft tofu, blended and flavored with salt and a little fresh parsley, is a perfect stuffer for shells in place of ricotta cheese, and can be used in lasagne. Blend tofu with fresh lemon juice to make a sour cream substitute or whip it with sugar and a dash of lemon to make a substitute for whipped cream.

· INGREDIENT GLOSSARY ·

Most of the recipes in this book use familiar ingredients that you'll find on your local supermarket shelves. But there are some special items that may be new to your kitchen. You'll find that using these in cooking will help you to create more interesting dishes.

Almond Butter: Almonds that have been puréed into a paste. You can make your own by grinding almonds in a food processor until a creamy butter forms, or you can purchase it in a natural foods store.

Balsamic Vinegar: An aromatic Italian vinegar made from grapes. It has a sweeter flavor than most vinegars.

Barley Malt Syrup: A sweetener made from sprouted barley. It's about half as sweet as sugar.

Basmati Rice: A very aromatic long-grain rice that is common in India and Pakistan. When cooked, it tends to be fluffier than other long-grain rice, but any long-grain white rice can be substituted for this.

Cilantro: The fresh green leaves of the coriander plant. Cilantro is also called fresh coriander or Chinese parsley and is common in the cuisine of Asian countries and also in Mexican dishes. It has a wonderful pungent and unique flavor. You won't find dried cilantro, since it doesn't keep its flavor when dried.

Couscous: A north African grain that is actually a quick-cooking form of wheat. It's made from the same type of wheat as pasta and cooks up to resemble very tiny pearled versions of pasta.

Eggless Mayonnaise: This is usually made from tofu and is a close imitation of authentic mayonnaise. You can make your own using our recipe on page 106. Or purchase a commercial brand. We recommend Nayonaise brand.

Flax Seed: Tiny seeds of the flax plant. These are sometimes added to baked goods, but we find them indispensable as an egg substitute (see page 21).

Kelp: A sea vegetable, usually sold in powdered form. Use as a condiment to give dishes a salty, briny flavor.

Miso: Fermented soybean paste that usually also contains a grain (barley or rice). Use as a condiment to add a deep, rich salty flavor to soups and other dishes.

Nutritional Yeast: A nutrient-rich inactive yeast. It doesn't have any leavening power, but rather adds nutrition and a "cheesy" flavor to dishes. Available in powdered or flake form.

Quinoa: An ancient grain, originally grown by the Incas in what is now Peru.

Soy Milk: A milk made by expressing the liquid from soaked soybeans. Regular and low-fat versions are available and some types are fortified with calcium and vitamin D.

Sun-Dried Tomatoes: Tomatoes that have been dried. You'll find them as plain dried tomatoes in a bag or immersed in olive oil in a jar. The plain ones need to be rehydrated with hot water before they are used. They have a strong flavor so that a little bit goes a long way.

Once you have experimented with sun-dried tomatoes in recipes, you will never want to be without them.

Tahini: Sesame seed butter made by blending raw or roasted sesame seeds.

Tempeh: A rich-tasting, fermented soybean cake. This is a staple in Indonesian cooking and makes a wonderful meat substitute in chili or on the grill.

Tempeh Bacon: A commercial imitation bacon made from tempeh.

Texturized Vegetable Protein· A high-protein dehydrated product made from soy flour. Rehydrated, it has a texture very similar to ground beef and is good in tomato-based dishes like tacos, chili, sloppy joes, and spaghetti sauce.

Tofu: Also referred to as bean curd, this is made by curdling soy milk and then pressing the curds into a solid block. Tofu has a bland flavor and takes on the flavor of other ingredients with which it is cooked. For this reason, it is a very versatile food that can be used in savory entrées or can be blended with sweetener to make desserts. When it is baked with seasonings and soy sauce, tofu produces a firm, chewy, flavorful commercial product that makes a good sandwich stuffer.

Vegetable Stock or Broth: Broth made from simmered vegetables. You can also purchase vegetable broth powder or cubes. Use in place of chicken broth in recipes.

Vegetarian Worcestershire Sauce: Worcestershire sauce that does not contain anchovies and is usually lower in sodium. Angostura Low-sodium is one brand that is vegetarian.

· USEFUL COOKING EQUIPMENT ·

Pressure Cooker: We're both big fans of the pressure cooker. In fact, we guarantee that once you've cooked with one, you won't be able to imagine how you got by without it. These pots cook beans and grains in a fraction of the time it takes with standard stove-top methods. As a result, they are a boon to the busy cook and also represent an environmentally sound way to cook foods. And nowadays, there is no reason to worry about exploding pots and potatoes on the ceiling. The new pressure cookers are perfectly safe.

Hand-Held Blender: This is so much more efficient than a regular blender. Just plug it in, dip it into a pot of food, and give it a few whirs to purée ingredients or produce a chunky soup. Then rinse it off under running water for fast clean-up. By partially puréeing soups and other dishes, you get a rich creamy consistency without added fatty ingredients, so this handy kitchen tool can help you to reduce fat in your diet while it makes your life easier.

CHAPTER THREE

Soups, Salads, and Sandwiches

Vegetable Stock

. . . .

A good vegetable stock forms the basis for many wonderful vegetarian dishes. This one is adapted from a recipe developed by chef Jay Brinkley and dietitian Mary Clifford for a vegetarian cooking class offered at Community Hospital of Roanoke Valley in Roanoke. Simmer the stock down until it is rich and concentrated, then freeze in ice cube trays and store the cubes in plastic zipper bags so you will always have some on hand. This is really two recipes in one. Once the stock is finished cooking, strain out the vegetables and purée them with soy milk and additional herbs to make a savory cream of vegetable soup.

1 teaspoon olive oil

1 large onion, peeled and chopped

2 celery ribs, chopped

½ cup chopped mushrooms

3 potatoes, peeled and diced

3 carrots, peeled and chopped

1 leek, sliced

6 parsley sprigs

1 bay leaf

2 fresh thyme sprigs, or 1 teaspoon dried

8 cups cold water

Heat the oil in a large saucepan. Add the onion, celery, and mushrooms and sauté for 2 minutes. Add the rest of the ingredients except the water. Sauté for 5 minutes. Add the water and bring to a boil. Reduce heat to low and simmer for at least 2 hours.

★ MAKES 8 CUPS

Cranberry Soup

. . . .

The winner of our $500 prize for best healthy holiday recipe is this wonderful cranberry soup created by Suzanne Essick of Silver City, New Mexico. It is so versatile you can serve it for almost any holiday. Heated, it makes a delightful warming starter for a festive Thanksgiving meal or holiday buffet. Served cold, the slightly tart flavor is wonderfully refreshing for those hot weather backyard picnics. You won't find fresh cranberries at your grocery store in the summer months, but this soup is equally tasty when you use dried cranberries. A bonus of this soup—it tastes deliciously rich although it is nearly fat-free and is loaded with vitamin C, fiber, and beta carotene.

3 cups fresh cranberries, or 2 cups dried
½ cup coarsely chopped onions
2 cups shredded carrots
1 cup coarsely chopped celery
1 cup water
4 cups vegetable broth
½ cup applesauce
½ cup frozen orange juice concentrate
½ teaspoon cinnamon
⅛ to ¼ teaspoon cloves
1 to 4 tablespoons brown sugar (use the smaller amount
*   if using dried cranberries)*

If you are using dried cranberries, soak them in 2 cups hot water for 15 minutes. Then drain; save the liquid and add to the soup. Combine the cranberries, onions, carrots, and celery with the water. Simmer uncovered for 30 minutes, or until all the water is gone. Add the remaining ingredients and pour into a blender. Blend until mixture is desired consistency. (If you purée it quite fine, the tastes blend well and one ingredient doesn't stand out more than the other.)

    Serve either hot or cold. Garnish with minced chives. In the summer you can add any small flowers, such as Johnny-jump-ups, calendula petals, chive blossoms, or basil flowers.

★ SERVES 6

Corn Chowder

. . . .

This easy soup is rich and hearty. Serve it with a salad and a loaf of bread for a simple meal that is filling and satisfying.

1 large onion, coarsely chopped
1 garlic clove, minced
1 green pepper, coarsely chopped
½ cup chopped celery
1 tablespoon olive oil
6 medium potatoes, diced
2 cups vegetable stock
2½ cups fresh or frozen corn kernels
2 cups plain soy milk
½ teaspoon sage
½ teaspoon rosemary
½ teaspoon basil
Salt and pepper to taste

Sauté the onion, garlic, green pepper, and celery in the olive oil for 2 minutes. Add the potatoes and vegetable stock and simmer over low heat until the potatoes are tender. Add the corn kernels, soy milk, and herbs and simmer for an additional 5 minutes. Season with salt and pepper.

★ SERVES 6

Soups, Salads, and Sandwiches

Potato Vegetable Soup

. . . .

This is a comforting cold-weather soup. Served with our soda bread, page 46, it makes a wholesome, nourishing meal.

2 large garlic cloves, pressed or minced
2 medium onions, chopped
2 teaspoons olive oil
5 cups vegetable broth or bouillon
3 medium russet potatoes, peeled and cubed
3 celery ribs, sliced
2 large carrots, peeled and sliced
1 medium zucchini, halved lengthwise and then sliced
1½ cups shredded cabbage
1 teaspoon dried dill weed
1 teaspoon dried tarragon
Salt and freshly ground black pepper to taste
Dried mashed potatoes sprinkled into soup to thicken to
*   desired consistency (optional)*
Chopped fresh chives for garnish

In a large soup pot, sauté the garlic and onions in the oil until translucent. Add broth, potatoes, and other vegetables. Simmer gently for 20 minutes, or until potatoes are tender. Add herbs, salt and pepper, and thickener if desired. Simmer soup an additional few minutes. Garnish with chives.

★ SERVES 6

Curried Potato and Onion Soup

. . . .

This quick and easy-to-make soup has added zest from curry powder and cumin. It is equally delicious served hot or cold.

2 teaspoons olive oil
2 large garlic cloves, pressed or minced
2 medium onions, chopped
1½ teaspoons ground cumin
1 teaspoon ground turmeric
1½ teaspoons curry powder, or to taste
Dash of black pepper
4½ cups vegetable broth or bouillon
2 to 3 cups peeled and diced potatoes
¾ cup plain soy milk
Salt to taste
Chopped fresh chives or cilantro for garnish

In a large soup pot, sauté the garlic and onion in the oil until transparent. Add spices and ¼ cup broth; stir well and cook for 5 minutes. Add the potatoes and remaining broth. Simmer gently for 20 minutes, or until potatoes are soft. Purée in batches in a food processor or use a hand-held blender and blend until smooth.

If serving cold, refrigerate for at least 6 hours.

★ SERVES 6

Spicy Squash Soup with Salsa

. . . .

Salsa with soup? We think you'll enjoy the combination of a thick creamy soup with the added spiciness of fresh salsa dolloped on top. This soup is delicious served either hot or cold. Warm corn bread is a tasty accompaniment.

❦ **SOUP**

1 to 2 teaspoons olive oil

2 medium carrots, sliced

2 large garlic cloves, minced

2 large onions, coarsely chopped

1 tablespoon flour

3 cups vegetable broth or bouillon

1½ pounds yellow squash, chopped

1 large boiling potato, peeled and diced

1 teaspoon Dijon mustard

1 to 2 teaspoons Mexican seasoning, or 1½ teaspoons chili
   powder plus ½ teaspoon ground cumin

2 cups frozen corn kernels

½ to 1 cup chopped red, yellow, or orange bell pepper

½ cup plain soy milk

1½ teaspoons fresh lime or lemon juice

❦ **SALSA**

1 large ripe tomato, peeled, seeded, and chopped

3 to 4 finely chopped green onions, including some of the
   green tops

1 teaspoon red wine vinegar

1 small jalapeño pepper, seeded and minced, or 2
   tablespoons canned

¼ cup chopped cilantro

Combine the salsa ingredients and refrigerate for at least an hour before serving.

To prepare the soup, heat olive oil in a large soup pot and sauté the carrots, garlic, and onions for about 5 minutes. Stir in flour and cook an additional 30 seconds. Gradually add the broth and stir well. Add squash, potato, mustard, spices, and 1 cup of corn. Simmer gently for 20 minutes, or until potatoes are soft. Purée in batches in a food processor or use a hand-held blender and blend until smooth. Bring to a simmer and add the rest of the corn, chopped sweet pepper, soy milk, and lime juice. Cover and cook 5 minutes. Top the center of each serving with a heaping tablespoon of salsa and chopped chives or additional cilantro.

If serving cold, refrigerate for at least 6 hours.

★ SERVES 6

Oli's Chili Soup

· ·

This wonderful spicy chili soup was one of the many delicious recipes
sent to us via the Internet when we announced the Healthy Holiday
Recipe Contest on the various food-related news groups. This recipe
comes from Oliver King-Smith of Berkeley, California, who said that it
was created by Melanie King-Smith for a special holiday—his birthday!

Don't let the list of ingredients deter you, this soup is definitely
worth making.

½ pound tofu

1 cup red chili or kidney beans

3 tablespoons extra-virgin olive oil

½ onion, chopped

2 tablespoons paprika

2 teaspoons turmeric

2 teaspoons salt

1 teaspoon chili powder

½ teaspoon hot red pepper flakes

1 teaspoon whole caraway seeds

½ teaspoon oregano

¼ teaspoon cayenne

¼ teaspoon ground ginger

Pinch of ground cloves

1 14½-ounce can diced tomatoes

1 10-ounce box frozen corn kernels

2 teaspoons Louisiana hot sauce

1 tablespoon tomato paste

3 cups vegetable stock, preferably homemade

1 cup bean stock

Freeze the block of tofu. Soak the red beans overnight. Throw away
the bean water. Boil the beans in 8 cups of water until they are soft,

about 2 hours. Drain the beans, but save 1 cup of the bean stock to flavor the chili.

Defrost the tofu and squeeze out all the liquid. Cut and shred the tofu into thin chunks. Fry the tofu in 2 tablespoons of olive oil until browned. Set aside.

In a Dutch oven, sauté the chopped onion in 1 tablespoon of olive oil. Add the spices and the fried tofu and sauté for 5 minutes. Add the remaining ingredients and reduce the heat. Simmer for 1 or more hours, stirring occasionally. The consistency will still be soupy. Garnish with chopped cilantro and a wedge of lime.

★ SERVES 6

Mushroom Barley Soup

This mushroom barley soup can be dressed up for company with the addition of wild rice, in fact the barley can be replaced totally with either brown or wild rice. Whichever way you choose, this is a flavorful, wholesome soup that's sure to be a favorite with everyone.

1 cup raw barley, wild rice, brown rice, or a combination
    of each
6 cups vegetable broth or bouillon
1 large onion
5 to 6 carrots, sliced (2 cups)
1 tablespoon olive oil
2 large celery ribs, sliced
1 tablespoon dried dill weed
4 cups sliced mushrooms
1 tablespoon low-sodium soy sauce
Freshly ground black pepper to taste
Minced fresh parsley for garnish

In a large soup pot, bring vegetable broth or bouillon to a boil; add barley or rice and bring to a simmer. Cover and cook until the barley is tender, about 40 minutes. If using wild rice, it will need at least 20 minutes more cooking; it should split open and curl back slightly when properly cooked.

In a large pan, sauté the onions and carrots in olive oil until the onions are soft, then add celery and dill weed. When lightly browned, add to soup pot. In same pan, sauté the mushrooms and add to soup pot.

Let mixture simmer gently for 25 minutes. Add soy sauce and pepper and more broth, if needed. To make a creamier soup, add ½ cup soy milk; heat thoroughly. Before serving, sprinkle with chopped parsley.

★ SERVES 8

Beet Salad

Debra Wasserman, co-coordinator of the Vegetarian Resource Group and cookbook author, offers this perfect Passover salad in her book, *The Lowfat Jewish Vegetarian Cookbook*. It is pretty, simple to make, and combines the unique flavors of horseradish and dill.

4 cups grated or finely chopped cooked fresh beets
2 teaspoons prepared horseradish
2 tablespoons balsamic vinegar
2 tablespoons frozen orange juice concentrate
2 tablespoons finely minced fresh dill

In a large bowl, mix all the ingredients together. Chill and toss once before serving.

★ SERVES 4

Haroseth

No Passover seder would be complete without this simple salad of nuts and fruit. It represents the mortar that the Jewish slaves used to build pyramids for the pharaohs.

8 apples, peeled and chopped
⅔ cup almonds or walnuts, coarsely chopped
½ teaspoon cinnamon
4 tablespoons sweet red Passover wine (or enough to moisten the ingredients completely)
1 or more tablespoons sugar to taste

Toss all ingredients together.

★ SERVES 8

Soups, Salads, and Sandwiches

Oregon Tuscan Salad

. . . .

Here is a tasty offering from Steve Altshuld of Portland, Oregon. Fennel, which looks somewhat like celery and has a delicate, mild licorice flavor, is one of the main ingredients in this delicious salad. Although dried herbs can be used, the addition of fresh herbs is especially appealing.

1 small fennel bulb, thinly sliced
½ pound fresh green beans, ends trimmed and cut into
*   1-inch lengths*
2 medium carrots, sliced
1 15-ounce can cannellini or small white beans
4 cups mixed salad greens torn into large bite-size pieces
2 tablespoons olive oil
2 large garlic cloves, pressed
1 to 2 tablespoons Dijon mustard
4 tablespoons balsamic vinegar
¼ cup water
6 scallions, sliced
1 tablespoon minced fresh thyme (if possible, use lemon
*   thyme; if not available, add 1 teaspoon grated lemon*
*   rind) or ½ teaspoon dried thyme*
2 tablespoons minced fresh basil, or 2 teaspoons dried
Freshly ground black pepper to taste
2 tablespoons coarsely chopped fresh parsley

Place fennel, green beans, and carrots in a steaming basket and steam until just tender, 7 to 8 minutes. Set aside to cool.

While vegetables are steaming, drain the cannellini beans; clean and dry the mixed salad greens. Clean and chop the herbs and set aside.

Combine the oil, garlic, mustard, vinegar, water, and scallions and mix thoroughly.

Assemble the salad by arranging the greens in a large bowl. Combine the beans and vegetables in a separate bowl, toss with the herbs (leaving the parsley aside), then add the dressing and pepper. Toss gently and spoon the mixture into the middle of the greens. Sprinkle with the chopped parsley.

★ SERVES 4

Carrot and Raisin Salad

. . . .

Here is a delicious, light rendition of an old favorite. Made with just a couple of teaspoons of oil and raspberry vinegar instead of mayonnaise, this carrot salad is a refreshing accompaniment to any meal.

1 pound carrots
2 teaspoons canola oil
Juice from 1 large lemon
1 tablespoon raspberry vinegar
½ cup raisins
1 tablespoon roasted sunflower seeds

Grate or shred carrots. Mix together oil, lemon juice, and vinegar and pour over carrots. Add raisins, mix well, and let sit at least an hour. Sprinkle with roasted sunflower seeds before serving.

★ SERVES 4

Notuna

This chickpea salad has a texture and taste that is reminiscent of tuna salad. Kelp powder, a sea vegetable, gives this dish its tuna flavor.

4 cups cooked chickpeas, or 2 16-ounce cans, well drained
½ cup coarsely chopped celery
½ cup finely chopped onion
2 tablespoons fresh lemon juice
½ cup eggless mayonnaise
1 tablespoon dried, powdered kelp
Salt and pepper to taste

Place the chickpeas in a food processor and process until coarsely chopped. Transfer to a bowl. Add the rest of the ingredients and mix. Serve stuffed into pita pockets with chopped tomatoes and lettuce.

★ 6 SANDWICHES

Tofu Sandwich Spread

Here is a lovely sandwich filling that is somewhat reminiscent of egg salad. Pile it onto whole wheat bread with sliced tomato and lettuce or stuff it into a pita pocket.

1 pound firm tofu
1 tablespoon finely chopped onion
¼ cup finely chopped celery
3 tablespoons eggless mayonnaise
1 tablespoon sweet pickle relish
1 teaspoon prepared mustard
¼ teaspoon dried dill weed

1 tablespoon dried parsley
Salt and pepper to taste

Cut the tofu into 4 slices and press each one firmly between paper towels to remove excess water. Then mash the tofu coarsely with a fork. Stir in the onion and celery. Combine the remaining ingredients and mix into the tofu.

★ SERVES 4

Submarine Sandwiches

. . . .

A good sub sandwich includes whatever you like. Here we've suggested using one of the wonderful savory baked tofu products that are found in the produce section of many supermarkets. Vary the other ingredients to suit your own preference.

1 pound baked tofu
4 submarine sandwich rolls
Sliced onion
Sliced green pepper
Sliced tomato
Lettuce leaves
Pickles
1 tablespoon herb-flavored vinegar
2 tablespoon olive oil

Slice the baked tofu and spread slices in each of the rolls. Top with slices of vegetables. Whisk together the vinegar and oil and drizzle just a small amount into each sandwich.

★ SERVES 4

Soups, Salads, and Sandwiches

New Potato Salad

. . . .

Although fresh new potatoes and peas straight from the garden are especially delicious in this salad, small red-skinned potatoes and frozen tiny green peas are a fine substitute. Whether using fresh or frozen peas, add them just before serving to keep their bright green color.

1 pound red potatoes, unpeeled, cut into pieces about the size of walnuts

2 carrots, peeled, cut lengthwise, and then cut into small pieces

1 tablespoon balsamic or wine vinegar

2 tablespoons dry sherry

3 tablespoons eggless mayonnaise

1 teaspoon crushed dried tarragon

Salt and pepper to taste

½ cup uncooked green peas

1 tablespoon roasted sunflower seeds (optional)

2 tablespoons finely chopped green onions, some green tops included

Cook potatoes in boiling water until just tender, 12 to 15 minutes. Remove with a slotted spoon and let drain in a colander. Cook carrots in the potato water for 3 or 4 minutes and drain. Mix together vinegar, sherry, mayonnaise, tarragon, and salt and pepper and pour over potatoes and carrots. Mix well and let sit at least an hour. Stir in peas and sprinkle with chopped green onions and roasted sunflower seeds (optional) before serving.

★ SERVES 4

Tempeh, Lettuce, and Tomato

. . . .

Tempeh, with its rich flavor, is perfect in sandwiches.

8 ounces tempeh
1 tablespoon lemon juice
1 tablespoon olive oil
2 tablespoons tamari
2 tablespoons tarragon vinegar
1½ tablespoons dried herbs (try basil, thyme, rosemary,
    and oregano)
1 crushed garlic clove
Freshly ground pepper to taste
Sliced ripe tomato
Lettuce leaves
4 teaspoons eggless mayonnaise
8 slices of bread

Cut the block of tempeh into eighths and then slice each piece through the middle to make 16 thin sheets of tempeh.

In a small bowl, whisk together the lemon juice, olive oil, tamari, vinegar, herbs, garlic, and pepper. Pour this marinade over the tempeh slices and let marinate for 1 hour in the refrigerator. Pour tempeh and marinade into a skillet and sauté for 15 minutes, turning frequently until tempeh is browned on each side. Drain off excess marinade.

Assemble the sandwiches using 1 teaspoon of eggless mayonnaise for each sandwich and layering the tempeh, lettuce, and tomato.

★ SERVES 4

Cranberry Fruit Relish

. . . .

This relish combines the tartness of cranberries with the sweetness of fresh fruits. Walnuts add a pleasant crunch. Serve it at your next holiday dinner.

3 cups fresh cranberries
2 medium apples, cut into chunks
Sections from 3 medium navel oranges
½ cup raisins
¼ cup maple syrup
¼ cup chopped pecans

Combine the cranberries, apples, oranges, and raisins in a food processor and process until mixture is chopped. Place in a bowl and add the maple syrup and chopped nuts. Mix well.

★ SERVES 8

Irish Soda Bread

. . . .

Soda bread, which requires no yeast or kneading, is quick and easy to make. You can bake it in a loaf pan or, for a crustier loaf, pat it into a rounded shape and bake on a cookie sheet. Feel free to experiment with whatever herbs or spices you like. We have offered two variations, a slightly sweet loaf with aniseed and raisins and an herbed loaf with sun-dried tomatoes and basil. This is a dense bread, best eaten the day it is made, but is also tasty toasted.

1 teaspoon cider vinegar or lemon juice (to sour the soy milk)
1¾ cups soy milk, at room temperature or slightly warm
1½ cups whole wheat flour

1½ *cups unbleached flour*
1 *tablespoon sugar*
1 *teaspoon baking powder*
½ *teaspoon baking soda*
½ *teaspoon salt*

Preheat the oven to 350 degrees. Lightly grease an 8 × 4-inch bread pan or cookie sheet. Pour the vinegar or lemon juice in the bottom of a 2-cup measuring cup, add the soy milk, and set aside to thicken and curdle slightly.

In a large bowl, stir together all the dry ingredients. Add milk and mix well. Dough will be stiff; continue to mix until it is smooth and sticky.

Press into pan or form a rounded mound and place on cookie sheet. Bake for 45 minutes. Cool on a rack and let sit for 10 to 15 minutes before slicing.

★ MAKES 1 LOAF

Soda Bread with Aniseed and Raisins

To the above ingredients, add 1 teaspoon aniseed and ½ cup raisins. Use either vanilla soy milk or add 1 teaspoon vanilla extract to mixture.

Basil and Sun-Dried Tomato Soda Bread

To the basic recipe, add 1 tablespoon crushed, dried basil, ½ teaspoon fennel, and ⅓ cup sun-dried tomatoes snipped with scissors into small pieces. (If you use the tomatoes not packed in oil, you will need to reconstitute them in 1 cup boiling water. Let sit at least 1 hour and drain before adding to the batter.)

CHAPTER FOUR

Appetizers and Dips

Vegetable Walnut Pâté

Here is an easy and delicious pâté to serve with crackers or pita wedges.

> ½ cup finely chopped onion
> 3 tablespoons olive oil
> 2 cups (1 can) cooked green beans
> ½ cup eggless mayonnaise
> ¼ cup chopped walnuts
> 2 tablespoons dry white wine

Sauté onions in oil until soft. Combine all ingredients in a food processor and blend until soft.

★ SERVES 6

$\mathscr{M}$ushroom $\mathscr{P}$âté

• • • • • • • • • • • • • • • • • • •

This delicious pâté can be served as an hors d'oeuvre, sandwich filling, or, as a side dish with French bread, a perfect accompaniment to a soup and salad dinner.

*⅔ cup finely chopped green onions (include some
    green tops)*
1 celery rib, finely minced
1 tablespoon olive oil or sherry
5 cups diced mushrooms
¾ teaspoon dried mixed herbs or herbes de Provence
¼ cup tahini
2 tablespoons low-sodium soy sauce
1 10-ounce package Mori-Nu Silken Tofu
Freshly ground black pepper to taste
Dash of cayenne
1¼ cups whole wheat bread crumbs
½ cup chopped pecans (optional)

Sauté the green onions and celery in the oil until the onions are translucent. Add mushrooms and herbs and cook over low heat until the mushrooms are fairly soft. Place mushroom mixture along with rest of ingredients in a food processor and blend to desired consistency.

Oil a medium loaf pan. Cut a sheet of waxed paper that is several inches larger than the pan, line the pan with it, and then oil the paper. Spoon in the pâté and fold the waxed paper over the top. Bake at 400 degrees for about 1½ hours.

When the pâté has cooled, fold back the waxed paper, invert pan onto a large platter, and carefully peel away the paper.

★ SERVES 6 TO 8

Mockamole

If you long for your favorite south-of-the-border dip but don't want the fat of avocado, try this reduced-fat version of guacamole. You can use either green peas or green beans for part of the avocado. Green peas will give this dip a slightly sweet flavor that we found especially appealing.

1 avocado
2 cups cooked peas or 1 cup cooked green beans
2 tablespoons chopped onion
¼ cup salsa (more to taste)
2 tablespoons fresh lime juice
Salt to taste

Blend the avocado and peas or green beans together in a blender, until smooth. Stir in the onion and salsa. Just before serving, stir in the fresh lime juice and salt. Serve with baked tortilla chips.

★ SERVES 6

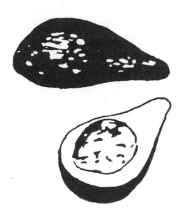

Baba Ganouj (Eggplant Pâté)

• • • • • • • • • • • • • • • • • • • •

Baba Ganouj is a popular Mideastern dip. It is traditionally prepared by first charring the eggplant, which gives it a pleasant smoky flavor. Or you can roast the eggplant in the oven and then impart additional flavor with a few drops of liquid smoke.

2 medium eggplants
Juice from 1 lemon
¼ cup tahini
3 garlic cloves
¼ cup finely chopped fresh parsley
1 teaspoon salt
¼ cup finely minced green onions
1 tablespoon olive oil
Dash of cayenne
1 or 2 drops liquid smoke (optional)

Wash the eggplants and prick them all over with a fork. Place on a cookie sheet and bake at 400 degrees for about 45 minutes, until they are soft and wrinkled. Cool and then scoop the insides into a food processor. Add the rest of the ingredients and process until smooth. Chill and serve with pita bread wedges.

★ SERVES 6

Stuffed Mushrooms

This deceptively simple recipe is a guaranteed hit at any party. Make these ahead and bake them just before serving.

1 pound fresh mushrooms
2 tablespoons olive oil
2 tablespoons minced onion
½ cup dry bread crumbs
½ teaspoon salt
¼ teaspoon paprika
⅛ teaspoon pepper

Preheat the oven to 400 degrees. Remove the stems from the mushroom caps and finely chop the stems. Sauté the chopped mushroom stems and minced onion for 5 minutes. Add the bread crumbs, salt, paprika, and pepper and sauté for 1 to 2 minutes more. Taste and adjust seasonings. Stuff the mushroom caps with this mixture. Place the caps in a nonstick baking pan and bake for 15 to 20 minutes, until the caps are tender.

★ SERVES 4

Appetizers and Dips

White Bean Dip with Fresh Ginger and Lime

. . . .

Minced ginger and fresh lime add a sparkling freshness to this low-fat bean dip. It is delicious with raw vegetables, crackers, or as a spread for crusty whole wheat bread.

> *3 cups cooked white, navy, or cannellini beans, or 2 cans drained rinsed beans*
> *1 tablespoon olive oil (optional)*
> *Zest and juice of 1 lime (scrape off the zest before you squeeze the juice)*
> *2 or 3 garlic cloves, peeled and minced or pressed through a garlic press*
> *1 1-inch piece fresh ginger root, peeled and minced*
> *2 to 3 green onions, minced (some green tops included)*
> *Dash of hot sauce*
> *¼ teaspoon salt (optional)*
> *3 tablespoons chopped cilantro*

In a blender or food processor, process the beans, olive oil, lime zest and juice, garlic, minced ginger, green onion, hot sauce, and salt until smooth. Transfer to a medium bowl and add chopped cilantro. Serve either chilled or at room temperature.

★ SERVES 6

CHAPTER FIVE

Entrées

Black Bean Chili

We have adapted this chili from a recipe by Lorna Sass, one of our favorite cookbook authors. Its full-bodied spiciness seems to improve if made the day before serving.

3 cans black beans, with the liquid of one
2 tablespoons Vogue Vegetable Broth plus ½ cup water
    or ½ cup vegetable bouillon
2 cups canned plum tomatoes, juice included
½ can chopped jalepeño chilies
1 large onion, coarsely chopped
1 teaspoon cumin seed
1 garlic clove, chopped or pressed
1 red bell pepper, seeded and chopped
1 tablespoon olive oil
1 to 2 tablespoons mild chili powder
1 teaspoon dried oregano
½ teaspoon whole fennel seed
¼ teaspoon cinnamon
2 to 3 cups water
½ cup tightly packed minced cilantro or parsley

Combine beans, broth, tomatoes and chilies in a large pot. In a frying pan, sauté the onion, cumin seed, garlic, and red pepper in the oil until slightly soft, then add chili powder, oregano, fennel seed, and cinnamon. Stir and add to bean mixture along with 2 cups of water. Simmer at least 20 minutes, adding more water if necessary; stir in about ⅓ cup cilantro. Serve in large soup plates over brown rice. Garnish with the rest of the cilantro, thin slices of avocado (optional), and a wedge of fresh lime.

★ SERVES 6

Kwanzaa Curried Rice Umoja

Kwanzaa is a Swahili word meaning "first fruit." It is a relatively new holiday created in the 1960s for African-Americans to celebrate their heritage and the values and principles that strengthen African-American families and communities. The holiday lasts seven days to coincide with the seven basic principles of Kwanzaa: unity, self-determination, responsibility, cooperative economics, purpose, creativity, and faith. The sixth night of Kwanzaa falls on New Year's Eve and is the traditional time for feasting and community gatherings. Because Kwanzaa is so new, it doesn't yet have traditional dishes, but the emphasis is on healthy foods, plant-based meals, and foods that are common in African and Caribbean cooking. Leonard Karlin, from Waterloo, Iowa, who submitted this recipe, notes that it includes ingredients that complement each other so well that this dish is symbolic of the Kwanzaa principle of "umoja," or unity.

¾ cup coarsely chopped onion

2 teaspoons curry powder

¾ teaspoon chili powder

1½ tablespoons peanut or olive oil

1½ cups long-grain or basmati rice

3 tablespoons raisins

½ teaspoon salt

3 cups water

1½ cups frozen sugar snap peas

1 red bell pepper, cut into ½-inch dice

1 yellow bell pepper, cut into ½-inch dice

¼ cup peanuts

In a large saucepan, cook the onion, curry powder, and chili powder in the oil over medium heat for 5 minutes, or until the onion is tender. Stir in the rice, raisins, and salt. Add the water. Heat to boiling; then reduce to medium-low heat. Cover and simmer for 15 minutes, or until the rice is tender and most of the water has been absorbed.

Stir in the sugar snap peas and the bell peppers. Cover and cook for an additional 5 minutes, or until the sugar snap peas and the bell peppers are tender. Serve garnished with the peanuts. (Or, as Leonard says, use your *uumba* (creativity) and garnish according to your *nia* (purpose).

★ SERVES 6

Sloppy Joes

. . . .

Texturized vegetable protein gives this dish a familiar meaty texture, but without any of the fat and cholesterol of ground beef.

1 tablespoon olive oil

1 cup coarsely chopped onions

2 medium green bell peppers, coarsely chopped

1½ cups boiling water

1 16-ounce can tomato sauce

1 tablespoon chili powder (more to taste)

1 teaspoon dried mustard

2 tablespoons brown sugar

1½ cups dry texturized vegetable protein (TVP)

Heat the oil and sauté the onions and pepper for 5 minutes. Add the remaining ingredients and simmer for 20 minutes. Serve over hamburger rolls.

★ SERVES 8

Entrées

Tempeh Stroganoff

• • • • • • • • • • • • • • • • • • •

Marinated tempeh stands in for the beef, and blended tofu makes a perfect sour cream substitute in this lower-fat version of an old family favorite.

1 pound tempeh
2 tablespoons fresh lemon juice
1 tablespoon water
1 tablespoon tamari
¼ tablespoon dry mustard
1 garlic clove, minced

1 pound silken tofu
4 tablespoons vegetable oil
2 tablespoons fresh lemon juice

½ cup sliced onion
2 tablespoons olive oil
1 pound mushrooms, thinly sliced
¼ teaspoon nutmeg
¼ cup dry white wine

1 pound pasta, cooked according to package directions

Cut the tempeh into thin strips and set aside. In a jar, combine the 2 tablespoons fresh lemon juice, water, tamari, mustard, and garlic. Shake to combine and pour over the tempeh. Let marinate for at least 2 hours in the refrigerator.

Place the silken tofu, vegetable oil, and 2 tablespoons lemon juice in a blender. Blend until puréed. Set aside.

In a large skillet, sauté the onions in the olive oil until they are transparent. Add the sliced mushrooms and sauté until they are

browned and tender. Add the marinated tempeh, the wine, and nutmeg. Sauté until the tempeh is browned and heated through. Remove
from heat and mix in the puréed tofu. Season with additional tamari.
Serve over pasta.

★ SERVES 4

Stuffed Squash

●　●　●　●　●　●　●　●　●　●　●　●　●　●　●　●　●　●

This is a lovely and festive dish for any holiday dinner. Prepare this
ahead by baking the squash and then stuffing it. Refrigerate overnight
and pop it into the oven a half hour before dinner is to be served.

2 medium butternut squashes

½ cup boiling water

¼ cup raisins

½ cup coarsely chopped onion

½ cup coarsely chopped celery

2 cups sliced mushrooms

2 tablespoons olive oil

¼ cup chopped walnuts

2 cups herb-flavored stuffing mix

¾ cup vegetable broth

Split the squashes in half lengthwise. Place split side down on a cookie
sheet and bake for 30 minutes at 350 degrees.

While squash is baking, pour the boiling water over the raisins
and set aside. Sauté the onion, celery, and mushrooms in the olive
oil until the onions are transparent. Add the walnuts and sauté for 1
to 2 minutes more. Add the stuffing mix and vegetable broth. Drain
the raisins and add these to the mixture.

Scoop the seeds out of the squash and fill with the stuffing mixture.
Bake for 25 minutes at 350 degrees.

★ SERVES 6

Entrées

Super Chili

. . . .

Dr. Neal Barnard, president of the Physicians Committee for Responsible Medicine, recommends this easiest of chili recipes. It is always a hit with both vegetarians and the most ardent of meat eaters.

1 cup boiling water

1 cup dry texturized vegetable protein

2 16-ounce cans whole tomatoes, chopped

1 3-ounce can tomato paste

1 large onion, coarsely chopped

1 green bell pepper, chopped

1 jalapeño pepper, minced

2 tablespoons chili powder (more to taste)

2 teaspoons cumin powder

2 teaspoons garlic powder

1 teaspoon dried oregano

¼ teaspoon allspice

1 cup cooked or canned kidney, pinto, or black beans

Pour the boiling water over the texturized vegetable protein and let sit for 5 minutes. Combine with remaining ingredients except the beans and simmer, covered, for 1 hour. Add the beans and simmer for an additional 30 minutes. Serve over rice or, for an interesting change, over spaghetti. This chili tastes even better when it is reheated the next day.

★ SERVES 8

Chow Mein

. . . .

This vaguely Chinese dish is traditionally served over crispy noodles. If it is served over rice, it is usually called chop suey. Serve it either way and vary the vegetables to suit your preferences.

1 tablespoon vegetable oil
2 medium onions, halved and thinly sliced
1 cup sliced celery
2 cups green beans, cut into 1-inch segments
1 cup sliced mushrooms
1 green pepper, seeded and sliced
1½ cups vegetable stock
3 tablespoons tamari
1½ teaspoons molasses
1 cup mung bean sprouts
⅔ cup slivered almonds
2 teaspoons cornstarch
1 tablespoon water
2 teaspoons sherry

Heat the oil in a large deep skillet and sauté the onions and celery for 5 minutes. Add the beans, mushrooms, and green pepper and sauté for an additional minute. Add the stock, tamari, and molasses. Cover and simmer for 10 minutes. Add the bean sprouts and almonds. Cover and simmer for an additional minute or two. Combine the cornstarch, water, and sherry to make a smooth mixture and add to the vegetables. Cook, stirring, until the mixture thickens.

★ SERVES 4

Vegetable Pot Pie

. . . .

Pot pies are comfort food at their best. There are no rules about what belongs in them, so they are a super way to use leftover vegetables. Our recipe offers the option of using tofu for a hearty dish, but you can omit it and use additional potatoes for a pot pie that is a bit lower in fat and faster to make. You can also shorten your preparation time a bit by using a prepared pie crust.

❧ PIE CRUST:

3½ cups unbleached flour

4 teaspoons baking powder

1 teaspoon baking soda

4 tablespoons margarine

1½ cups plain soy milk

1 tablespoon barley malt

❧ FILLING:

1 pound firm tofu

¼ cup unbleached flour

½ teaspoon black pepper

½ teaspoon garlic powder

2 tablespoons nutritional yeast

¼ cup oil

½ cup thinly sliced carrots

½ cup thinly sliced celery

1 cup coarsely chopped onions

2 cups diced potatoes

3 cups vegetable stock

½ cup peas, fresh or frozen

1 teaspoon sage

½ teaspoon thyme

3 tablespoons unbleached flour
Salt and pepper to taste

For the pie crust, sift the flour, baking powder, and baking soda together into a bowl. With a pastry blender, cut the margarine into the flour mixture until it resembles coarse corn meal. Mix together the soy milk and the barley malt and add to the flour mixture. Stir with a fork to form a stiff dough. Mix with hands if necessary. Divide the dough in half and turn out onto a floured surface. Roll into two crusts.

Press the tofu firmly to get rid of excess water. Cut it into ½-inch cubes. Combine the flour, pepper, garlic powder, and nutritional yeast. Toss the tofu cubes in this mixture to coat them well. Heat the oil in a skillet and sauté the tofu until it is browned. Drain off the excess oil. Add the carrots, celery, onion, potatoes, and 2¾ cups of the vegetable stock. Cover and simmer for 20 minutes, or until vegetables are tender. Add the peas and the sage and thyme.

In a small bowl, whisk together the 3 tablespoons of flour with the remaining ¼ cup vegetable stock. Stir into the vegetables and tofu and simmer until a thick gravy forms. Season with salt and pepper.

Pour into an unbaked pie shell and place a pie crust layer over the top. Seal the edges of the crusts and prick several times with a fork. Bake at 350 degrees for 30 minutes.

★ SERVES 6

Entrées

Madras Vegetable Curry

• • • • • • • • • • • • • • • • • • • •

This recipe is a very happy "special occasion" memory for Polly Knappen of Pacifica, California. She says: "When we were children and were allowed to have any meal we wished—on our birthdays or whatever other special occasion—each of us would choose this household curry. My mother had gotten the recipe from one of her best friends, who had spent a number of years working in India for the World Health Organization, cataloguing 700 different curries. This household curry from the state of Madras was her favorite. Ours, too."

We know you will love this curry as much as Polly's family did. It is a lovely combination of spicy curry flavor, with a tang of lemon offset by the sweetness of apples and bananas. Truly an unusual curry, it is one of the best we've tasted.

1 cup unsweetened shredded coconut

1 cup water

1½ cups plain soy milk

3 tablespoons olive oil

1 cup coarsely chopped yellow onion

2 to 4 tablespoons curry powder (depending on how hot you like it)

¼ teaspoon cinnamon

¼ teaspoon allspice

¼ teaspoon ground cloves

¼ teaspoon ground nutmeg

1 heaping tablespoon currant jelly

1 lemon, seeded and chopped, including the skin (pare off the ends of the skin a bit if it is especially thick)

1 apple, cored, peeled, and thinly sliced

2 carrots, thinly sliced

2 zucchini or yellow summer squash, sliced into ½-inch pieces

2 white potatoes, peeled and cut into chunks

½ head cauliflower, cut into small florets
¼ pound green beans, cut into 2-inch lengths
2 bananas
Shredded coconut for garnish
Fresh lemon juice

Combine the coconut, water, and soy milk and bring to a boil. Remove from heat and let stand 30 minutes. Strain the coconut, pressing it with the side of a spoon to get all the coconut "milk" out. Reserve the liquid and discard the coconut (or refrigerate it to add to cake batter or cookie dough).

Heat the olive oil and sauté the onions until they are transparent. Stir in the curry powder, spices, currant jelly, and chopped lemon. Cook over low heat for 5 minutes. Add the coconut liquid and stir thoroughly. Add all remaining ingredients except the banana.

Bring to a boil, then lower heat and cook over medium-low heat, covered, for about 25 minutes, until the potatoes are tender. You may need to stir it occasionally. Slice one banana and add to the curry. Cook for an additional 10 minutes. Serve over rice and garnish with shredded coconut and thinly sliced banana that has been sprinkled with lemon juice. For best flavor, make this dish ahead of time. Let the curry cool for a couple of hours before adding the banana. Then add banana, reheat, and serve.

★ SERVES 6

Starving Artists' Banquet

• •

This delicious dish from Marjorie Groff of Boyertown, Pennsylvania, makes a beautiful presentation of vibrantly colored food. It will be a perfect edible centerpiece for your holiday table. Serve it for winter holidays or for Easter.

1 pound black beans

1 pound yellow saffron rice

3 tablespoons olive oil

2 large onions, coarsely chopped

3 garlic cloves, minced

Juice and grated rind of 3 oranges

⅓ cup Marsala wine or dry red wine

½ tablespoon sugar

½ teaspoon dried oregano

4 ounces pimientos, drained and chopped

Fresh chopped parsley

Soak beans in 8 cups water. Drain and discard the water. Place beans in a large pot and add water to cover. Simmer until beans are tender, 1½ to 2 hours (or cook in a pressure cooker for 10 minutes). Drain the beans and reserve the cooking liquid. While beans are cooking, prepare the saffron rice according to package directions.

In the olive oil, sauté the onion and garlic until tender. Drain and discard the oil. Add the orange juice and rind, wine, and sugar. Add enough of the reserved bean cooking liquid to cover. Simmer for 20 minutes. Add oregano and pimientos and simmer for an additional 10 minutes.

Edge a large round platter with a ring of fresh parsley. Within the ring, make a hollow nest of the cooked saffron rice. Fill the center of the nest with the black beans.

★ SERVES 10

Potato Pancakes

. . . .

Potato pancakes, or potato latkes, are a popular Hanukkah tradition. Traditional recipes call for several eggs to hold the pancake together. We use a cholesterol-free lower-fat binder of tofu blended with white flour.

4 ounces soft tofu

2½ tablespoons unbleached flour

2 cups grated raw potatoes (peel the potatoes first)

1 teaspoon salt

3 tablespoons grated onion

1 tablespoon dried parsley

Blend the tofu and the flour together in a blender or food processor until smooth and well mixed. Place in a bowl and add the rest of the ingredients. Mix thoroughly. Drop spoonfuls onto a hot well-oiled skillet. Cook until brown; flip and cook until second side is browned and crisp. Serve immediately with applesauce.

★ SERVES 4

Entrées

Stuffed Cabbage

· ·

The humble cabbage was once a vegetable in such demand that, in ancient Rome, only the rich could afford to eat it. Today, it is enjoying a resurgence in popularity since it is believed to contain a chemical that helps to prevent cancer. This recipe is adapted from one served in cafeterias that participate in a culinary adventure called the Gold Plan—a program of good nutrition and wonderful vegetarian food sponsored by the Physicians Committee for Responsible Medicine.

1 small head cabbage

⅔ cup raisins or currants

2 teaspoons olive oil

1 onion, coarsely chopped

½ pound mushrooms, chopped

¼ teaspoon nutmeg

⅛ teaspoon garlic powder

¼ cup chopped parsley

Dash of pepper

¼ cup chopped walnuts

Salt to taste

3 cups cooked rice (white or brown)

4 cups tomato sauce

¼ cup sliced mushrooms

Remove the core from the cabbage. Steam for 5 minutes and then carefully peel off the leaves and set aside to cool.

Pour 1 cup boiling water over the raisins and set aside.

Heat the olive oil in a large skillet and sauté the onions and chopped mushrooms (not the sliced ones) until the onions are transparent. Drain the raisins and add them to the skillet along with the nutmeg, garlic powder, parsley, pepper, walnuts, and salt. Stir in the rice and 1 cup of the tomato sauce. Remove from heat. Pour 1 cup tomato sauce over the bottom of a 9 × 12-inch baking dish. Spread a cabbage leaf on a flat surface and spoon about ⅓ to ½ cup of the rice mixture into the center of the leaf. Roll the leaf firmly and place seam side down in the baking pan. Follow with the rest of the cabbage leaves. When the pan is filled, pour the remaining tomato sauce over the top of the rolls and top with the sliced mushrooms.

Cover and bake at 350 degrees for 45 minutes. You can also make this ahead and keep in the refrigerator. In this case, bake for 1 hour.

★ SERVES 6

Black Bean Burritos

• • • • • • • • • • • • • • • • • • • •

This is a quick, easy-to-fix supper that can also serve as a nutritious lunch in place of a sandwich.

1 16-ounce can black beans, rinsed and drained

1 package Fantastic Foods Black Beans, prepared as directed

12 corn or wheat tortillas (at room temperature or warmed, they won't split when rolled)

½ cup finely chopped red onion

½ cup chopped red or green pepper

Salsa

1 small can jalapeño peppers (optional)

Chopped cilantro (optional)

Add the drained black beans to the black bean mixture and mix well. On each tortilla, spread some of the bean mixture in the center, sprinkle with chopped onions, red pepper, and a tablespoon or two of salsa (and optional cilantro and jalapeño peppers.) Fold the bottom of the tortillas up a couple of inches and then roll up lengthwise. These can be heated briefly in a microwave.

★ SERVES 6 to 12

Entrées

Mexican Pumpkin Stew

. . . .

Linda Arcadia of Moscow, Idaho, created this spicy soup with the rich flavors of autumn. She suggests that for a festive fall meal, you can serve this in a scooped out pumpkin.

3 to 4 cups of small chunk (½-inch) raw pumpkin or
*   butternut squash*
1 cup vegetable stock
1 medium onion, thinly sliced
1 teaspoon minced garlic
1 cup tomato sauce
½ cup salsa
1 16-ounce can corn kernels, drained
1 teaspoon chili powder
½ teaspoon cumin
3 to 4 drops of Tabasco (optional)
½ teaspoon hot red pepper flakes
1 15-ounce can red kidney or pinto beans
Salt and pepper to taste

Simmer the pumpkin or squash in the vegetable stock until tender. Add the remaining ingredients and simmer uncovered over low heat for 30 minutes. Season with salt and pepper.

★ SERVES 6

Lasagne

· ·

Blended tofu and spinach create a rich-tasting filling for this special homemade lasagne.

½ pound fresh mushrooms

2 teaspoons olive oil

2 28-ounce cans plain prepared spaghetti sauce

12 ounces lasagna noodles

1 10-ounce package frozen chopped spinach, thawed

1 pound soft tofu

¼ cup chopped fresh parsley

½ teaspoon salt

Slice the mushrooms and sauté in the olive oil until tender. When they are completely cooked, add the spaghetti sauce and set aside.

While the mushrooms are cooking, cook the lasagna noodles according to package directions. Drain and set aside.

Drain the excess water from the thawed spinach and place in a food processor. Add the tofu, parsley, and salt. Process until thoroughly blended.

Preheat the oven to 350 degrees.

Spread half the sauce on the bottom of a 9 × 12-inch casserole dish. Cover with a layer of cooked noodles. Spread half the tofu-spinach mixture over this. Cover with another layer of noodles, the rest of the tofu-spinach mixture, and a final layer of noodles. Pour the remaining tomato sauce over this. Cover tightly with foil and bake for 30 minutes until completely heated through.

★ SERVES 8

Garbanzo-Cashew Loaf

. . . .

This healthy loaf from Ruth Cornelius of Elmhurst, New York, has fast become one of our favorite recipes. It is especially good cold; make it a day ahead and it tastes like a fine vegetarian pâté. It is a wonderful addition to any picnic served with crusty French bread.

2 cups rolled oats

2 tablespoons wheat bran

2 cups water

3 tablespoons low-sodium soy sauce

1 teaspoon Italian herb blend or any kind of fresh herbs from your garden

1 teaspoon dried parsley, or 1 tablespoon fresh

1 cup chopped celery

1 cup chopped onions

2 garlic cloves, chopped

1 cup chopped mushrooms (optional)

1 tablespoon olive oil, or 2 tablespoons water

1 16-ounce can garbanzos

¼ cup water

¼ cup sliced ripe olives (optional)

½ cup of premeasured cashews ground fine

In a large mixing bowl, combine the oats, bran, and 2 cups of water, soy sauce, and herbs. Sauté until tender the celery, onions, garlic, and mushrooms in oil or water. Then whirl garbanzos in a blender with ¼ cup water to turn blender easily. Add all ingredients to oatmeal mixture and combine thoroughly. Spray a casserole with oil, spread the pâté, and bake in a 350-degree oven for about 1 hour.

★ SERVES 8

Fruits of the Harvest Pasta

• • • • • • • • • • • • • • • • • • • •

Here is another offering for Kwanzaa; this comes from Mary Kayaselcuk of Newport News, Virginia. This is a colorful, tasty meal all-in-one. It's low in fat, high in fiber, and easy to make. If you are not having a crowd, divide the recipe and freeze half.

12 to 14 manicotti shells

1 10-ounce package frozen chopped spinach, thawed and drained

1 16-ounce can pinto beans

1 14½-ounce can Italian-style stewed tomatoes

¾ cup chopped onions

½ cup chopped red pepper

2 cups cooked brown rice

½ cup medium salsa

Black pepper and garlic salt to taste

1 26-ounce can or jar of light spaghetti sauce with mushrooms

¼ cup minced parsley for garnish (optional)

Boil manicotti shells in water for 8 minutes. Drain and cool. Combine spinach, beans, tomatoes, onions, red pepper, brown rice, salsa, black pepper, and garlic salt.

Spread about 1 cup of the tomato sauce in the bottom of a large casserole (or two smaller 9 × 13-inch ones). Split the manicotti open lengthwise, place on top of the sauce, and abundantly fill with bean mixture; fold up the sides and place tightly together in the dish. Cover with the remaining sauce. Bake, covered, for 20 minutes at 350 degrees, remove the top, and bake an additional 10 minutes, or until piping hot. Add parsley before serving.

★ SERVES 8 TO 10

Teriyaki Vegetables with Couscous

• • • • • • • • • • • • • • • • • •

This delicious and easy-to-prepare recipe comes from Claudia Demick of Barrington, Rhode Island, who says that it is "perfect for a family New Year's Eve supper, with the added bonus that any leftover vegetables become New Year's Day lunch. Just heat the vegetables and serve them in pita pockets or rolled into warmed flour tortillas."

❦ TERIYAKI SAUCE
⅓ cup low-sodium soy sauce
1 to 2 tablespoons brown sugar
2 tablespoon dry sherry
1 garlic clove, minced
1 to 2 teaspoons minced fresh ginger

❦ VEGETABLES
½ pound fresh mushrooms, quartered
½ red pepper, sliced into strips
½ yellow pepper, sliced into strips
½ large onion, halved and sliced
¾ cup cauliflower florets
¾ cup broccoli florets
1 15-ounce can garbanzo beans, drained

❦ COUSCOUS
2¼ cups water
½ teaspoon salt
1½ cups whole wheat couscous
½ teaspoon cumin seed (optional)

Combine all ingredients for the teriyaki sauce in a large bowl. Add the vegetables to the sauce. Preheat the broiler. Bring water to a boil for the couscous. Stir in salt, couscous, and cumin seed. Lower heat, cover, and cook until water is absorbed, 12 to 15 minutes. Fluff with a fork.

Pour vegetables and marinade into a large shallow pan. Broil until vegetables are tender but still crisp, about 5 minutes. Stir and broil an additional 3 to 5 minutes. Mound couscous on plates making a well in the center. Spoon vegetable mixture onto the couscous.

★ SERVES 4

𝒯*acos*

. . . .

1 cup texturized vegetable protein
⅞ cup boiling water
½ cup coarsely chopped onion
1 tablespoon olive oil
1 cup tomato sauce
1 cup cooked pinto beans
2 teaspoons chili powder
1 teaspoon ground cumin
8 corn or flour tortillas
Chopped tomatoes
Shredded lettuce
Salsa

Pour the boiling water over the texturized vegetable protein and set aside. In a large skillet, sauté the onion in the olive oil until transparent. Add the texturized vegetable protein, tomato sauce, pinto beans, chili powder, and cumin. Mix well and simmer for 20 minutes.

Warm the tortillas in the oven or on a griddle. Fill each tortilla with about ½ cup of the taco filling and top with chopped tomatoes, shredded lettuce, and salsa.

★ SERVES 4

Entrées

Hoppin' John

. . . .

Although this spicy dish is a traditional New Year's Day offering in the South, we think it's too good to save for just once a year. If you can, make it the day before; the flavors meld and are definitely enhanced by a rest overnight in the fridge.

4 cups cooked black-eyed peas (1½ cups dried),
*   or 2 16-ounce cans, drained*
2 cups vegetable broth (we recommend Vogue Vegetable
*   Broth)*
3 to 4 tablespoons olive oil
1 cup each: chopped onions, chopped carrots, chopped red
*   pepper, sliced celery*
2 garlic cloves, minced
¼ teaspoon cayenne (or more to taste)
½ cup coarsely chopped green olives
1 to 2 tablespoons balsamic vinegar
Salt and freshly ground black pepper to taste

Put cooked black-eyed peas in a large pot with the vegetable broth. In a frying pan, heat olive oil and sauté onions and garlic a few minutes. Add carrots, pepper, and celery. Stir, cover, and simmer gently for 5 minutes. Add vegetables, cayenne, chopped olives, and vinegar to black-eyed pea and broth mixture. Mix well, cover, and cook an additional 10 to 15 minutes; add salt and pepper to taste. Serve with additional hot sauce for those intrepid fans who enjoy really spicy food.

★ SERVES 6

Peppers Stuffed with Quinoa

• • • • • • • • • • • • • • • • • • •

Sweet red or yellow peppers can be used for this recipe. Quinoa, an unusual quick-cooking grain, makes a nice change-of-pace stuffing for these peppers (you can also use long-grain brown rice.)

1 large onion, finely chopped
1½ tablespoons olive oil
2 garlic cloves crushed
2 large tomatoes, peeled and chopped
1¼ cups quinoa
1 teaspoon cinnamon
2¼ cups water
Salt and freshly ground black pepper
6 bell peppers, with a good squarish shape
2 tablespoons chopped parsley
1 teaspoon dried mint
¼ cup each dried apricots and currants
¼ cup roasted pine nuts (optional)

Sauté the onion in oil. Add garlic, tomatoes, and quinoa and cook gently, stirring often, for 3 to 4 minutes.

Add the cinnamon, water, and a teaspoon of salt. Bring to a boil, then cover the pan and cook very gently for 15 minutes.

Meanwhile, cut the peppers in half lengthwise and scoop out the seeds. Parboil the peppers in 1 inch of water for 5 minutes. Drain and dry them on paper towels.

Preheat the oven to 350 degrees. Season quinoa mixture with pepper and more salt if necessary, stir in chopped parsley, mint, apricots, and currants, then spoon mixture into the pepper halves.

Put the peppers in a lightly oiled casserole. Bake for 25 to 30 minutes, until the peppers feel tender when pierced with a skewer. Top with roasted pine nuts if desired.

★ SERVES 6

Entrées

John's Three-Bean Stew

• • • • • • • • • • • • • • • • • • •

Perfect for a cold winter evening, this hearty, easy-to-make stew was created by our friend, John Futhey, of Port Townsend, Washington. Its rich-tasting but low-fat flavor is enhanced by a hint of molasses and balsamic vinegar. As leftovers, it's great served over brown rice.

3 medium yellow onions

2 garlic cloves, minced

2 tablespoons olive oil

3 vegetable bouillon cubes

1 cup boiling water

1 tablespoon balsamic vinegar

½ teaspoon paprika

½ teaspoon salt

Pepper to taste

2 tablespoons molasses

3 or 4 carrots

3 or 4 medium potatoes

1 29-ounce can crushed tomatoes

1 15-ounce can black beans

1 15-ounce can white beans

1 15-ounce can black-eyed peas

Chop the onions, place in a stew pot, and add minced garlic and olive oil. Cook until translucent and light brown in color. Dissolve bouillon cubes in the boiling water and add to onion mixture. Add balsamic vinegar, paprika, salt, pepper, and molasses and stir. Cut carrots and potatoes into 1-inch chunks and add to the pot. Add the tomatoes and beans, making sure to add the liquid the beans are packed in. (Alternatively, you may start with dried beans and cook them in your usual way and use them instead of canned beans.)

Cook over medium-low heat until the potatoes and carrots are tender.

★ SERVES 8

Shepherd's Pie

There are probably hundreds of different shepherd's pie recipes—
every family seems to have its own. Basically it's a thick, hearty,
stewlike concoction with a topping of mashed potatoes. Start with our
basic recipe and add whatever leftover vegetables you have. A cup
of beans such as garbanzos or a half pound cubed tofu are also delicious
additions. Miso, a fermented bean paste, makes a very flavorful gravy;
try the light or "white" miso for a somewhat more delicate taste.

1 large onion, peeled and chopped

1 to 2 garlic cloves, minced

2 teaspoons olive oil, or ¼ cup dry sherry

2 carrots, chopped into ½-inch pieces

*2 small to medium zucchini, halved lengthwise and cut into
    ½-inch pieces*

2 to 3 cups mushrooms, stemmed and cut into quarters

1 tablespoon low-sodium soy sauce

1 to 2 tablespoons light miso mixed with ½ cup hot water

*5 to 6 cups mashed potatoes (commercial potato flakes made
    according to directions with soy milk substituted for
    regular milk are quick and easy)*

Preheat the oven to 350 degrees.

Sauté onions and garlic in oil or sherry until soft. Add the vegetables and mushrooms and cook until crisp-tender. Add soy sauce and
miso and water, stir well, and heat through. Put the vegetable mixture
in the bottom of a 9 × 13-inch casserole and top with the mashed
potatoes. Bake uncovered until the filling is hot and bubbly, 20 to 25
minutes.

★ SERVES 4

Capirotada
(Mexican Christmas Bread Pudding)

• • • • • • • • • • • • • • • • • • • •

Some holidays, like Thanksgiving, Passover, and the Fourth of July, have traditional dishes that are easily recognized as a part of that celebration. But Christmas, celebrated throughout the world, is likely to have family traditions depending on the family's own cultural background. This unusual dish, offered by Rose Geiger of Cosby, Tennessee, is a traditional part of Mexican Christmas dinners. It is a delightfully unique combination of sweetness offset by the savory flavors of fresh cilantro and soy cheese.

Mexican cooks use a type of brown sugar that comes in a cone, called *panocha*, to sweeten this dish. If you can find this ingredient at an international food store, do use it, but dark brown sugar is a good substitute. Although the predominant flavor is a sweet one, Rose says that this bread pudding is usually served along with the main course of Christmas dinner. We agreed that it works well as a side dish and is especially nice alongside spicy dishes, such as those that might be served at a Mexican Christmas dinner.

16 slices whole wheat bread

¾ cup panocha *or dark brown sugar*

4 cups water

1 stick cinnamon, crushed

¼ cup sweet onion

¼ cup chopped peanuts

1 cup raisins

1 Delicious apple, diced

¼ cup chopped fresh cilantro

6 ounces soy cheese (we suggest VeganRella brand cheese)

Toast the bread and tear into bite-size pieces. Place them in a large shallow baking dish. In a large saucepan, mix brown sugar, water, and crushed cinnamon. Bring to a boil and boil gently over medium-high heat for 30 minutes. Strain the syrup, removing the cinnamon.

Combine the onion, nuts, raisins, apple, and cilantro and mix lightly into the bread. Pour the brown sugar syrup over the bread mixture and toss lightly to coat the bread. Grate the soy cheese and spread it over the top of the bread. Push it gently into the bread mixture. Bake at 375 degrees, uncovered, for about 30 minutes. Serve warm.

★ SERVES 12 TO 16

Entrées

Valerie's Summer-Easy Baked Beans

· · · · · · · · · · · · · · · · · ·

Equally great for a Fourth of July picnic or a blustery evening's supper are these baked beans from Valerie Parker, good friend and wonderful low-fat cook. The beans are rich in flavor, but a snap to prepare; easy too to double the recipe for a crowd.

2 15-ounce cans pinto beans, rinsed and drained
½ cup chopped onion
2 tablespoons molasses
1 teaspoon Angostura Lite Worcestershire sauce
2 tablespoons cider vinegar
1 teaspoon Dijon mustard
2 tablespoons chili sauce
⅛ teaspoon garlic powder
½ cup tomato sauce

Preheat the oven to 350 degrees. Combine all ingredients in a 1-quart casserole, cover, and bake for 1 hour.

★ SERVES 4

Fresh and Easy Tomato Sauce

· · · · · · · · · · · · · · · · · ·

This is one of our favorite sauces and a snap to make—our only advice is, don't bother unless you can get really tasty, homegrown, fresh tomatoes. Fresh basil, although not imperative, makes the sauce especially flavorful. Serve it over pasta or rice or use it as a "bed" on which to steam fresh green beans.

1 tablespoon olive oil
1 large onion, peeled and chopped

2 garlic cloves, peeled and minced
6 to 8 medium tomatoes, peeled and coarsely chopped
(no need to seed unless you want to)
¼ cup tightly packed fresh basil, finely chopped,
or 1 tablespoon dried basil
Salt and pepper to taste

In a large frying pan, sauté the onion and garlic in olive oil. When slightly brown, add chopped peeled tomatoes. (To make peeling easier, with a slotted spoon place the tomatoes in boiling water for about 20 seconds, the skin will now slip off readily.) Bring tomato mixture to a simmer, add basil and salt and pepper and cook slowly, covered, for about 20 minutes. If the sauce seems too soupy, remove the lid for the last 5 minutes of cooking.

★ MAKES 3 CUPS

★ SERVES 2 TO 4

Vegetables

Orange and Fennel Green Beans

· ·

Although Steve Altshuld of Portland, Oregon, created this refreshing salad for Thanksgiving, we think it's delicious anytime of the year. If fresh fennel is not available, you can get a similar taste by substituting ½ to ¾ cup thinly sliced celery and ½ teaspoon dried fennel seeds.

¾ pound green beans, cut into 1- to 2-inch lengths
1 small fennel bulb, trimmed and thinly sliced
  (about ½ cup)
1 tablespoon olive oil
¼ cup orange juice
¼ to ½ cup walnuts, pecans, or pistachio nuts
1 large shallot, thinly diced, or 1 small sweet onion,
  such as Vidalia, Walla Walla, or Bermuda
1 to 2 tablespoons finely chopped fresh tarragon,
  or 1 teaspoon dried tarragon
Salt and pepper to taste
1 orange, peeled and separated into sections, then cut into
  bite-size pieces.
1 tablespoon white wine vinegar or raspberry vinegar

Parboil or lightly steam the trimmed beans until just tender.

Prepare the fennel bulb by cutting it crosswise into thin slices. Place in a medium bowl.

Add beans to fennel and toss them with the oil, juice, nuts, shallot or onion, and tarragon. Season to taste with salt and freshly ground black pepper. Add the orange slices and toss gently. Just before serving, mix in the vinegar. (Adding the vinegar too soon will acidify the beans turning their color from bright green to olive drab.)

★ SERVES 6

Mama Bellini's Steamed Asparagus with Garlic and Lemon

· ·

This recipe calls for large tender stalks of peeled asparagus. If you haven't tried peeling asparagus, do; it's really worth the effort. It makes it incredibly tender and needs far less cooking than if it's left unpeeled. Use asparagus that is about the diameter of your thumb or larger.

> 2 large garlic cloves, minced
> 2 teaspoons olive oil
> Juice of half a lemon
> 1 teaspoon grated lemon peel
> ¼ cup vegetable broth
> 1 teaspoon dried tarragon
> 8 large stalks of peeled asparagus (break off bottom tough white parts)

In a small frying pan with a tight fitting lid, sauté garlic in oil, but don't let it brown. Add lemon juice, lemon peel, vegetable broth, and tarragon; mix well. Arrange the asparagus in a single layer on top of the broth mixture, cover pan, and steam gently. Check frequently and cook just until tender. Do not overcook. The asparagus should not be mushy.

★ SERVES 2

Oven-"Fried" Potatoes

· ·

These tasty low-fat French fries are easy to make. You can season them any way you like, but our friend Mary Clifford uses chili powder to give them a nice punch.

3 pounds medium baking potatoes
1 tablespoon vegetable oil
1 to 2 teaspoons chili powder

Preheat the oven to 425 degrees. Coat a large rimmed baking pan with vegetable cooking spray. Cut each potato in half lengthwise, then cut each half lengthwise into quarters. In a large bowl, toss together potatoes, oil, and chili powder until the potato wedges are well coated. Spread potatoes on a greased pan in one layer. Bake for about 20 minutes, or until nicely browned.

★ SERVES 8

Creamed Spinach

• • • • • • • • • • • • • • • • • • • •

Creamed spinach is a rich, satisfying dish that lends itself to many uses. Use your imagination. Serve it as a vegetable or thin it with a little soy milk to make a sauce for grains. Chop some black olives or sun-dried tomatoes into it along with a few leaves of fresh basil and then toss it with hot pasta. You might also vary the greens in this dish. Instead of spinach, try kale or Swiss chard.

1 pound fresh spinach, or 1 10-ounce package frozen
chopped spinach
1 cup Low-Fat White Sauce (page 107)
Dash of nutmeg

Place the spinach in a covered saucepan with ¼ cup water and simmer for 5 minutes (or cook frozen spinach according to package directions). If using fresh spinach, place it in a food processor and process just enough to chop it. Put in a bowl and mix in the white sauce until well combined. Add the nutmeg.

★ SERVES 4

Sweet and Sour Vegetables

. . . .

¾ cup vegetable stock
1 tablespoon cornstarch
1 20-ounce can pineapple chunks, drained
    (reserve the liquid)
1 tablespoon tamari
¼ cup apple cider vinegar
¼ cup firmly packed brown sugar
1 tablespoon vegetable oil
2 cups halved mushrooms
1 cup broccoli florets
½ cup pea pods
1 medium carrot, thinly sliced
1 green pepper, halved and thinly sliced
½ cup slivered almonds

In a small bowl, whisk together ¼ cup of the vegetable stock and the
cornstarch until it is free of lumps. Add ½ cup of the reserved pineapple
juice, tamari, vinegar, and brown sugar. Set aside.

In a large skillet, heat the oil. Add the mushrooms, broccoli, pea
pods, carrots, and green pepper and sauté for 5 minutes. Add the remaining vegetable stock. Cover and cook over low heat for 10 minutes.
Add the pineapple chunks, the cornstarch mixture, and the almonds and
cook over low heat, stirring until the sauce is thick and bubbling.

Serve over rice.

★ SERVES 4

Green Beans with Tempeh Bacon

. . . .

This recipe from Cherie Soria of Bend, Oregon, calls for tempeh bacon
(see Glossary). Try Light-Life Fakin' Bacon, found in the freezer or

refrigerator section of most natural food stores. Its smoky flavor imparts a good old-fashioned taste to the green beans. Chopped spinach or chard could be used instead of beans.

1 pound fresh or frozen green beans
1 quart water, plus 1 teaspoon salt
1 to 2 teaspoons olive oil
1 large onion, peeled and chopped
2 garlic cloves, minced
4 ounces tempeh bacon, cut into ½-inch slices

Blanch beans in salted boiling water for 5 minutes. Drain.

Heat a skillet to medium and add oil. Sauté onions, garlic, and "bacon" until golden. Add drained beans to onion mixture, cover, and cook until beans are tender.

★ SERVES 4 TO 6

Carrots in Love

. . . .

Joni Hilton, from Cedar Rapids, Iowa, sent us this easy-to-prepare vegetable dish that is sure to be popular with any age. It would be a pleasant addition to a traditional Thanksgiving dinner.

8 medium carrots, peeled and sliced
3 bananas, peeled and sliced
½ cup orange juice, or ⅓ cup orange juice
*   and 2 tablespoons lemon juice*
½ cup white raisins
1 to 2 tablespoons minced fresh ginger (optional)
¼ cup sliced toasted almonds (optional)

Simmer sliced carrots in water until almost tender. Drain. Add bananas and juice and bring to a simmer again. Bananas will swell and then dissolve to form a sweet glaze. Just as carrots become cooked, add raisins and ginger. Stir to coat all ingredients and serve hot. Sprinkle with toasted almonds.

★ SERVES 6

Brussels Sprouts with Apple and Lemon Zest

. . . .

In France these are known as *petits choux,* or little cabbages, and that's exactly what they look like—miniature green cabbage heads. Apple, orange juice, and lemon zest add a delicate fresh flavor to the brussels sprouts. Be careful not to overcook.

2 cups fresh brussels sprouts cut in half
1 large firm apple (such as Granny Smith), peeled, cored,
*   and cut into eights*

Juice of a fresh orange, or ¼ to ⅓ cup frozen orange juice
1 teaspoon lemon juice
2 teaspoons lemon zest
½ tablespoon margarine
1 teaspoon sugar
½ to 1 teaspoon dried tarragon
Dash of salt

Combine all ingredients in a saucepan. Cover and simmer over low heat for 12 to 15 minutes, until just tender. For a crisper apple taste, add the apple the last 3 or 4 minutes of cooking.

★ SERVES 4

Vegetables

Spicy Collards with Ginger

· · · · · · · · · · · · · · · · · ·

Collards treated this way become soft, with an earthy freshness and a pleasing nippy bite.

1 pound collard greens, washed and cut into thin strips
2 cups vegetable broth
1 tablespoon olive oil
1 chopped onion
2 garlic cloves, pressed or minced
1 tablespoon minced fresh ginger (no need to peel, just
    rinse before mincing)
1 jalapeño, stem and seeds removed, minced (use rubber
    gloves when mincing the peppers!)
Black pepper to taste

Combine collards with broth in a nonaluminum pot. Simmer, covered, until tender, but not mushy. Timing will vary, but 35 minutes is average.

Heat 1 tablespoon of the olive oil in a large skillet and stir in onion and garlic. Soften slightly over moderate heat. Add ginger and jalapeño and stir for a moment. Add collards and stir over moderate heat until liquid has almost evaporated. Remove from the heat and stir in black pepper.

★ SERVES 4

Note: You can substitute turnip greens in this dish or combine a variety of greens for a particularly interesting effect: kale, collards, Swiss chard, mustard greens—any and all.

Sweet Potatoes with Apples and Ginger

. . . .

We agree with Irma Rombauer, the author of the classic *Joy of Cooking*, when she said she marveled "at any cook who voluntarily dwarfs the possibilities of a sweet potato with marshmallow!" This recipe is sweetened with only a small amount of brown sugar and orange juice, allowing the taste of the sweet potatoes and apples to hold their own.

6 medium or 4 large sweet potatoes, peeled and sliced
*   ¼ inch thick*
2 apples, cored and thinly sliced
¼ cup water
1 to 2 tablespoons finely chopped candied ginger
½ to 1 teaspoon orange zest
2 to 3 tablespoons brown sugar
Salt and pepper to taste
½ cup orange juice
1 tablespoon margarine (optional)

In a large pot of boiling water, simmer the sweet potato slices until almost tender. In a smaller pot, cook the apples in ¼ cup water until nearly done. Drain both potatoes and apples. Grease a 9 × 13-inch casserole and place half the sweet potatoes in it. Cover with the apple slices, chopped ginger, half the brown sugar, orange zest, and a dash of salt and pepper. Top with remaining sweet potatoes and brown sugar and pour the orange juice over all. Dot with margarine (optional). Cover with aluminum foil and bake at 350 degrees for 20 minutes.

★ SERVES 8

CHAPTER SEVEN

Gravies
and Sauces

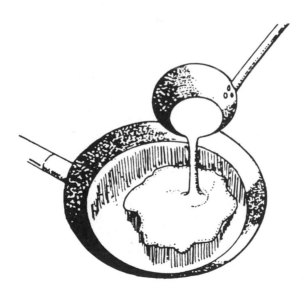

Chickpea Gravy

. . . .

Here is a simple, vegetarian gravy to serve over stuffing or mashed potatoes at your next holiday dinner.

1 small onion, chopped
2 tablespoons vegetable oil
2 tablespoons flour
1 cup chickpea stock (use water in which chickpeas were
*   cooked or liquid from canned chickpeas)*
½ teaspoon sull
¼ teaspoon dried marjoram
Dash of pepper
Dash of garlic powder

Sauté the onion in the oil until it is transparent. Stir in the flour and cook, stirring, for 2 minutes. Add the chickpea stock, pouring slowly and stirring to avoid any lumps. Allow the mixture to come to a boil. Lower heat and simmer until thickened. Add the marjoram, salt, pepper, and garlic powder.

★ MAKES 1½ CUPS

★ SERVES 6

Mushroom Almond Gravy

• •

Cherie Soria from Bend, Oregon, created this savory gravy, which is delicious over potatoes, vegetables, or grains.

1 tablespoon minced shallots
2 cups minced mushrooms
1 teaspoon olive oil
2 tablespoons almond butter
1½ tablespoons miso
¼ cup unbleached flour
2 cups water

Sauté the shallots and mushrooms in the olive oil until tender. Combine the almond butter, miso, flour, and water in a blender and blend until smooth and well mixed. Add to the mushrooms in the skillet and simmer until thick.

★ MAKES 3 CUPS

★ SERVES 12

Sweet French Dressing

• •

Homemade dressings give such a fresh taste to salads. French dressing is simple to make and is always a family favorite.

⅔ cup ketchup
½ cup sugar
⅔ cup vegetable oil
½ cup red wine vinegar
Salt to taste

2 garlic cloves, minced

2 tablespoons minced onion

Combine all ingredients in a jar with a tight-fitting lid and shake to combine.

★ MAKES 2 CUPS

Ranch Salad Dressing

. . . .

Here is a dairy and egg-free ranch dressing that is quite a bit lower in fat than commercial brands.

1 cup eggless mayonnaise

1 cup plain soy milk

1 tablespoon white vinegar

2 tablespoons finely chopped green onions

¼ teaspoon onion powder

2 teaspoons minced parsley

1 garlic clove, finely minced

¼ teaspoon paprika

⅛ teaspoon cayenne

¼ teaspoon salt

¼ teaspoon black pepper

Place all ingredients in a jar with a tight-fitting lid. Shake well to blend.

★ MAKES 2 CUPS

Eggless Mayonnaise

· · · · · · · · · · · · · · · · · ·

This recipe produces a wonderful creamy dressing for salads and sandwiches.

10½ ounces soft silken tofu
1 tablespoon white vinegar
1 tablespoon fresh lemon juice
½ teaspoon Dijon mustard
1 tablespoon vegetable oil
Pinch of salt

Place all ingredients in a blender and blend until smooth. Refrigerate overnight before using.

★ MAKES ABOUT 1 CUP

Thousand Island Dressing

· · · · · · · · · · · · · · · · · ·

Use eggless mayonnaise to produce a reduced-fat version of this popular salad dressing.

¾ cup eggless mayonnaise
1 tablespoon sweet pickle relish
2 tablespoons chili sauce or ketchup
2 tablespoons finely chopped green bell pepper
2 tablespoons finely chopped onion
1 tablespoon fresh lemon juice
½ teaspoon granulated sugar
¼ teaspoon vegetarian Worcestershire sauce

The Vegetarian No-Cholesterol Family-Style Cookbook

Combine all ingredients in a small bowl and mix thoroughly.

★ MAKES 1 CUP

Low-Fat White Sauce

• •

This simple sauce forms the basis for many rich-tasting dishes. Serve it as is over vegetables or blend it with cooked, puréed vegetables to make a sauce for grains, or a savory cream soup.

> *1 tablespoon margarine*
> *2 tablespoons flour*
> *1 cup plain, light soy milk*
> *Salt and white pepper to taste*
> *Grating of nutmeg*

Melt the margarine in a saucepan over low heat. Stir the flour in to make a thick paste and cook, stirring rapidly, for 1 minute. Pour the soy milk in very slowly, stirring to avoid lumps. Cook and stir with a wooden spoon over low heat for several minutes until the sauce is thick. Season with salt, pepper, and nutmeg.

★ MAKES 1 CUP

CHAPTER EIGHT

Desserts

*Brownies*

• •

These are a wonderful, rich, chocolaty brownie from the Texas Society for Animal Rights. They are a true indulgence; enjoy them for a special occasion.

2 cups unbleached flour
2 cups sugar
⅓ cup cocoa
1 teaspoon baking powder
½ teaspoon salt
1 cup water
1 cup vegetable oil
1 teaspoon vanilla extract
¼ cup chopped pecans or walnuts

Preheat the oven to 350 degrees.

Mix the flour, sugar, cocoa, baking powder, and salt in a large bowl. Mix together the remaining ingredients and add them to the flour mixture. Stir until well blended. Pour into a 9 × 13-inch pan and bake for 25 to 30 minutes. Let cool for 10 minutes before cutting into squares.

★ MAKES 16 BROWNIES

Carrot Cake

. . . .

Carrot cake is always a fun dessert. This version uses our flax seed egg replacer to produce a cholesterol-free version of an old-fashioned recipe.

> 1½ tablespoons flax seed
> ¼ cup water
> 1 cup sugar
> ½ cup vegetable oil
> 1 cup unbleached flour
> 1 teaspoon baking soda
> ½ teaspoon salt
> 1 teaspoon cinnamon
> 1¾ cups grated carrots
> ¼ cup walnuts, chopped

Preheat the oven to 350 degrees.

Place the flax seed in a blender and grind into a fine powder. Add the water and blend until slightly thickened. Mix together the sugar, oil, and flax seed mixture. Add the flour, baking soda, salt, and cinnamon. Stir in the carrots. Fold in the nuts. Pour into a 9-inch square baking pan and bake for 35 to 40 minutes.

★ SERVES 8

Fruit Compote with Cashew Cream

. . . .

Served warm with its delicately flavored sauce, this fruit compote is perfect for either brunch or a dinnertime dessert. It is reprinted, with permission, from *Quick Cuisine*, a wonderful small pressure cooker cookbook distributed by Kuhn-Rikon Corporation.

2 cups water
¼ cup maple syrup
½ pound mixed dried fruit
½ cup raisins
1 cup peeled and sliced carrots
¼ teaspoon ground cinnamon
2 teaspoons grated lemon rind
1 tablespoon arrowroot or cornstarch
½ cup cashews

Put water and syrup in a 2-quart or larger pressure cooker. Allow to come to a simmer over medium-high heat. Add dried fruit, raisins, carrots, cinnamon, and lemon rind.

Close lid and bring up to high pressure. Adjust heat to stabilize pressure. Cook for 5 minutes. Remove from heat and use quick-release method to release pressure. Remove fruit with a slotted spoon. Add arrowroot to remaining liquid and stir to mix. Bring to a simmer to thicken, stirring constantly. Place cashews and thickened liquid in the bowl of a food processor and process until ingredients are smooth (or purée in small deep bowl with a handheld blender).

Serve fruit in bowls topped with the cashew cream sauce.

★ SERVES 6

Note: If not using a pressure cooker, simmer ingredients on low heat for 20 to 30 minutes, until tender, then continue with above directions.

Chocolate Cake
with Chocolate Frosting

• • • • • • • • • • • • • • • • • • • •

It is hard to believe that this rich-tasting cake is relatively low in fat. It is sure to please any ardent chocolate fanatic with its intense chocolaty flavor and fine, moist, but light texture.

To make it almost totally fat-free, follow the Fat-Free Chocolate Cake variation and substitute a dusting of confectioners' sugar instead of the frosting.

1½ cups unbleached flour

3 tablespoons unsweetened cocoa powder

1 cup sugar

1 teaspoon baking soda

1 teaspoon salt

1 ripe banana, mashed or sliced

3 tablespoons vegetable oil

1 tablespoon vinegar

1 teaspoon vanilla extract

1 cup cold water

2 to 3 tablespoons raspberry jam (optional for filling)

Preheat the oven to 350 degrees.

Sift the flour, cocoa, sugar, baking soda, and salt together in a large mixing bowl. In a small bowl, combine the banana, oil, vinegar, vanilla, and water and beat until blended. Add to dry ingredients, blend well, and pour into an ungreased 9-inch cake pan or a 4 ½ × 8 ½-inch loaf pan. If you are going to use the raspberry jam filling, it is easier to cut the cake if you use a loaf pan.

For 9-inch pan, bake 25 minutes; for loaf pan, cook 35 minutes. Cool, if using the raspberry filling, cut the cake in two or three layers, spread with jam, and frost with Chocolate Cream Frosting.

Note: Using thread to cut the cake into layers will make the cuts even and clean. Encircle the cake with a two-foot piece of thread, making sure that it is even from the bottom all around, then pull the ends of the thread together until it has cut through the cake.

Chocolate Cream Frosting

• •

> 1¼ cups confectioners' sugar
> 2 tablespoons unsweetened cocoa
> 2 tablespoons margarine
> Dash of salt
> 1 teaspoon vanilla extract
> 2 tablespoons plain or vanilla soy milk

Cream together the sugar, cocoa, margarine, and salt. Add the vanilla and milk to make a creamy, spreadable consistency.

Fat-Free Chocolate Cake

• •

This variation will give you an almost totally fat-free cake. Although it is slightly denser, it is rich tasting, wonderfully chocolaty, with just a hint of banana flavor.

Use the above recipe but omit the oil and use a whole large (or 1½ medium) ripe banana, mashed. Instead of the frosting dust the cake when it is cool with confectioners' sugar. If you place a paper lace doily over the cake and sift the sugar over it, when you remove the doily you will have a pretty, decorative pattern.

Rice Pudding

. . . .

Rice pudding is one of those wonderful old-fashioned comfort foods that seems to have fallen out of favor, perhaps because it takes so long to cook the traditional way. But if you have a pressure cooker, be sure to try this quick, easy-to-make recipe for a delicious old-time treat. Warmed up leftovers are great for breakfast in place of hot cereal.

1½ cups vanilla soy milk or rice milk

2 cups water

1 cup basmati or jasmine white rice

1 teaspoon ground cinnamon

½ teaspoon ground cardamom

¼ teaspoon ground nutmeg

½ cup raisins or dried cranberries

Dash of salt

2 to 3 tablespoons liquid sweetener

In a pressure cooker, bring water, soy or rice milk, rice, spices, raisins, salt, and 2 tablespoons of the sweetener to a simmer. Lock the lid into place and bring to high pressure. Adjust heat to maintain high pressure for 4 minutes. Remove from heat and let pressure release naturally for 10 minutes. Remove lid and add remaining sweetener if needed and fluff with a fork. Serve warm or cooled with additional soy or rice milk and a spoonful of fruit syrup on top.

★ SERVES 6

Old-Fashioned Oatmeal Cookies

. . . .

¼ pound margarine

½ cup firmly packed brown sugar

¼ cup sugar
1 tablespoon soy flour
1 tablespoon water
½ teaspoon vanilla extract
¾ cup unbleached flour
½ teaspoon baking soda
½ teaspoon cinnamon
1½ cups rolled oats (or quick oats)
½ cup raisins

Preheat the oven to 350 degrees.

Beat together the margarine and sugars until creamy. Add the soy flour and water and beat well to blend.

In a separate bowl, combine the flour, baking soda, and cinnamon. Add to the margarine mixture and mix completely. Stir in the oats and raisins.

Drop by rounded teaspoonfuls onto ungreased cookie sheets. Bake for 10 to 12 minutes, or until light golden brown.

★ MAKES 24 COOKIES

Desserts

Peanut Butter Cookies

Peanut butter cookies are an old family favorite. But although they are a nutritious treat, they are notoriously high in fat. There won't be a truly low-fat peanut butter cookie until someone makes a low-fat peanut. Until then, this recipe offers a cookie that is quite a bit lower in fat than traditional recipes.

4 tablespoons margarine
½ cup firmly packed dark brown sugar
½ cup granulated sugar
⅔ cup reduced-fat peanut butter
¼ cup water
½ teaspoon vanilla extract
½ teaspoon salt
½ teaspoon baking soda
1 to 1½ cups unbleached flour

Preheat the oven to 375 degrees.

Cream together the margarine, sugars, and peanut butter. Add the water and vanilla and mix thoroughly. In a separate bowl, sift together the salt, baking soda, and flour. Add this dry mixture ¼ cup at a time to the peanut butter mixture. The dough will be very stiff. Form into balls the size of walnuts and place on a greased cookie sheet. Flatten with the back of a fork twice, turning the fork to make a crisscross design. Bake for 10 to 12 minutes, until browned.

★ MAKES 24 COOKIES

Date Bars

. . . .

Dates and oats make this an especially nutritious sweet treat. Buy chopped dates to speed up the preparation time.

5⅓ tablespoons margarine
½ cup brown sugar
½ cup soy milk
1 cup chopped dates
½ cup chopped walnuts
¼ cup unbleached flour
¼ teaspoon salt
½ teaspoon baking powder
1 teaspoon cinnamon
¼ teaspoon cloves
½ teaspoon allspice
¾ cup rolled oats

Cream together the margarine and brown sugar. Add the soy milk, dates, and walnuts and combine thoroughly. In a separate bowl, sift together the flour, salt, baking powder, cinnamon, cloves, and allspice. Add the rolled oats to the dry ingredients and mix together. Add the dry ingredients to the date mixture, mixing to combine thoroughly. Spread in an 8-inch square pan. Bake for 20 minutes.

★ MAKES 16 2-INCH BARS

Gingerbread Cake
with Lemon Hard Sauce

. . . .

Mary Clifford, a wonderful vegetarian cook, offers this quick and delightful gingerbread cake. A dab of peanut butter adds a rich but mellow flavor to an old-time favorite. Let this cake cool completely before slicing or it will be crumbly.

⅓ cup margarine

⅓ cup firmly packed dark brown sugar

1½ tablespoons peanut butter

¾ cup light molasses

2 cups unsifted all-purpose flour

1 tablespoon baking powder

1 tablespoon ground ginger

1 teaspoon cinnamon

½ teaspoon ground nutmeg

Pinch of salt

¾ cup water

❦ LEMON HARD SAUCE

1½ cups unsifted confectioners' sugar

4 tablespoons margarine, softened

2 tablespoons fresh lemon juice

1 teaspoon grated lemon peel

2 to 4 tablespoons vanilla soy or rice milk (enough to
    achieve a spreadable consistency)

Preheat the oven to 325 degrees. Grease and flour an 8-inch round cake pan.

In a large bowl, cream together the margarine brown sugar, peanut butter, molasses. Mix together flour, baking powder, ginger, cinnamon, nutmeg, and salt and stir into margarine mixture alternately with water until well combined. Pour batter into prepared pan. Bake about 40 minutes, or until cake tester or knife inserted in center comes out clean. Let cool completely on a wire rack. Meanwhile, prepare lemon hard sauce. In a small bowl, whisk together the confectioners' sugar, margarine, lemon juice, lemon peel and milk. Refrigerate until ready to serve. Stir before using.

★ SERVES 8

Desserts

Pumpkin Pie

. . . .

No Thanksgiving would be complete without this traditional dessert. We've deleted the eggs and milk from this one and added creamy, blended tofu for a pie that is less fatty and is especially rich tasting.

1 16-ounce can pumpkin
1 teaspoon cinnamon
½ teaspoon ginger
¼ teaspoon nutmeg
⅛ teaspoon ground cloves
½ teaspoon salt
1 teaspoon vanilla extract
1 cup light brown sugar
1 tablespoon molasses
¾ pound soft tofu
1 unbaked pie shell

Preheat the oven to 350 degrees.

Combine all ingredients except the tofu and pie shell in a blender and blend until mixed and completely smooth. Break the tofu into chunks and add to the pumpkin mixture. Blend well. Pour the filling into the pie shell. Bake for 1 hour. Chill completely before serving.

★ SERVES 8

Caramel Corn

. . . .

Here is an easy Cracker Jack-like snack. Use the greater amount of popcorn if you prefer a less sweet snack.

¾ cup packed brown sugar
4 tablespoons margarine

3 tablespoons corn syrup or other liquid sweetener
¼ teaspoon salt
¼ teaspoon baking soda
¼ teaspoon vanilla extract
8 to 12 cups popped popcorn
1 cup peanuts (optional)

Combine the sugar, margarine, corn syrup, and salt in a saucepan and cook over low heat until the margarine is melted. Then continue to cook (without stirring) for 3 minutes. Add the baking soda and vanilla. Pour over popcorn and peanuts and mix until evenly coated. Bake for 15 minutes at 300 degrees. Break into pieces.

Desserts

CHAPTER NINE

Breakfasts

Banana-Blueberry Pancakes

. . . .

Breakfast can be special any morning with these fast, easy pancakes.
Top with fresh fruit and maple syrup.

1½ cups unbleached flour

1 teaspoon salt

3 tablespoons sugar

2 teaspoons baking powder

1½ tablespoons flax seed

¼ cup water

1 tablespoon vegetable oil

1½ cups soymilk

1 medium banana, thinly sliced

1 cup fresh blueberries

In a large bowl, combine the flour, salt, sugar, and baking powder.
Place the flax seeds in a blender and blend at high speed until they
are completely ground. Add the ¼ cup water and blend on medium
for 1 minute, until the mixture is thick. In a separate bowl, combine
the flax seed mixture, vegetable oil, soy milk, sliced banana, and
blueberries. Pour into the dry mixture and mix with a few swift
strokes. Cook the pancakes on a hot griddle or nonstick frying pan
that has been lightly greased. Cook on one side for 3 to 4 minutes,
until small bubbles appear on the upper surface. Then flip one and
cook for an additional 2 minutes, or until the second side is browned.
Serve with fresh fruit, maple syrup, or applesauce.

★ MAKES 12 PANCAKES

Banana French Toast

• •

Blended bananas make a perfect batter for a slightly sweet, rich-tasting French toast.

2 very ripe bananas
1 cup plain soy milk
8 slices whole wheat bread

In a blender, blend the bananas and soy milk until completely smooth. Pour into a large bowl. Dip the bread in this mixture and then cook on a lightly oiled hot griddle until just browned on each side.

★ SERVES 4

French Toast

• •

Here is a recipe for a traditional family favorite, but without the fat and cholesterol that is found in old-fashioned versions of this dish. Ground flax seed blended with water is the secret here. It stands in for the eggs to make a perfect French toast batter.

3 tablespoons flax seed
½ cup water
1½ cups plain soy milk
8 slices whole wheat bread

In a blender, grind the flax seed into a fine powder. Add the water and blend until it is slightly thick. Add the soy milk and process just enough to blend. Pour into a large bowl. Dip the bread into the soy milk mixture and cook on a lightly oiled griddle or frying pan until browned on both sides.

★ SERVES 4

Apple Cinnamon Oatmeal

Nothing makes a cold morning cozier than a bowl of steaming oatmeal. Dress yours up with apples and cinnamon for a special treat.

> 2 cups rolled oats
> 3¼ cups water
> ¼ teaspoon salt
> ½ teaspoon cinnamon
> 1 cup coarsely chopped apples

Combine all ingredients in a saucepan. Bring to a boil. Lower heat and cook for about five minutes, stirring occasionally. Sweeten with brown sugar or maple syrup if desired.

★ SERVES 4

Breakfasts

Couscous with Cinnamon and Raisins
· ·

Couscous, the traditional dish from North Africa, is made from coarsely
ground durum wheat. Although it is most often served at dinnertime
with vegetables, we find it a delicious alternative to breakfast cereal.
The addition of raisins, bananas, and cinnamon make it a welcome,
comforting way to start the day.

> ¾ *cup water*
> ¼ *cup orange juice*
> ½ *cup whole wheat couscous*
> 1 *teaspoon orange zest (optional)*
> ¼ *cup raisins*
> ½ *ripe banana, thinly sliced*
> 2 *tablespoons apple juice concentrate*
> ¼ *teaspoon cinnamon*

Put all ingredients in a saucepan, stir, and bring to a boil. Lower heat,
cover, and cook for about 5 minutes. Let sit a few minutes, fluff with
a fork, and serve.

★ SERVES 2

Orange Ginger Muffins
· ·

These flavorful, delicious muffins are a treat anytime of the year. They
have a light, pleasing texture. For a lovely gift, tuck them into a small
basket lined with a pretty napkin.

> 1 *cup orange juice*
> ⅓ *cup maple syrup or other liquid sweetener*
> ⅓ *cup vegetable oil*

1 teaspoon vanilla extract

½ cup orange marmalade

1½ cups whole wheat pastry flour

1½ cups unbleached white flour

1 tablespoon baking powder

1 teaspoon baking soda

½ teaspoon salt

1½ to 2 teaspoons ground ginger

2 teaspoons orange rind

¼ cup candied ginger

Preheat the oven to 375 degrees.

Place the orange juice, sweetener, oil, vanilla, and marmalade in a blender and blend for about 30 seconds, until it is thoroughly mixed. (You can also place them in a bowl and blend with a hand blender.)

In a separate bowl, combine the flours, baking powder, baking soda, salt, ginger, and orange rind and mix thoroughly. Add the wet ingredients to the dry and combine with a few swift strokes. Add the candied ginger and stir just enough to distribute through the batter.

Fill greased muffin tins to the top. Bake for 20 to 25 minutes, until just golden brown.

★ MAKES 12 MUFFINS

Johnny Cakes

· ·

Also called hoe cakes and ash cakes, these are a traditional American breakfast taught to the English settlers by the Native Americans. No doubt, the first Johnny cakes didn't use tofu, but we find that a small amount of tofu blended with flour helps the batter to hang together. Serve them with real maple syrup for a traditional treat.

1 ounce soft tofu
1 tablespoon unbleached flour
¾ cup soy milk
1 cup cornmeal
½ teaspoon salt

In a blender, blend the tofu and flour until it is smooth. Add the soy milk and blend just to mix. Pour into a bowl. Add the cornmeal and salt. Drop by spoonfuls into a well-oiled skillet. Cook until golden brown. Then flip them over and cook until second side is golden brown.

★ SERVES 4

Spiced Pumpkin Pancakes

· ·

These unusual spiced pancakes are perfect for a weekend brunch. Top them with thinly sliced fresh fruit such as peaches, strawberries, or even bananas, and hot maple syrup.

½ cup canned puréed pumpkin
½ cup yellow cornmeal
½ cup unbleached flour
¼ cup brown sugar
1 teaspoon baking powder

¼ teaspoon salt
½ teaspoon pumpkin pie spice
1 teaspoon grated orange peel
2 teaspoons finely chopped candied ginger (optional)
¼ cup water
1 tablespoon vegetable oil
¾ cup plain or vanilla soy milk

Combine pumpkin with the dry ingredients. Mix water, oil, and soymilk and add to pumpkin mixture. Beat just until smooth. Heat griddle or frying pan and oil lightly. Use about ¼ cup of batter for each pancake; cook until bubbles appear, then turn. Remove when pancakes are golden and slightly firm to the touch.

★ SERVES 4 TO 6

Strawberry Smoothie

• • • • • • • • • • • • • • • • • •

Here is a thick and creamy shake that's a great, quick, and easy way to start your morning or a refreshing way to cool off on a hot summer's day. It's always a hit with kids, too.

1 frozen banana, cut into chunks (peel and wrap banana
    in plastic wrap before putting in freezer)
½ cup frozen strawberries or a mixture of berries and other
    fruit
½ cup vanilla soy milk
2 tablespoons strawberry or other fruit syrup
3 ice cubes

Place all ingredients in a blender and blend on high speed until smooth and creamy.

★ SERVES 2

Breakfasts

Holiday Menus

• THANKSGIVING •

Vegetable Walnut Pâté with crackers
Stuffed Squash
Mashed potatoes with Mushroom Almond Gravy or Chickpea Gravy
Brussels Sprouts with Apple and Lemon Zest
Sweet Potatoes
Cranberry Fruit Relish
Pumpkin Pie

• HANUKKAH •

Potato Pancakes with applesauce
Mushroom Barley Soup
Stuffed Cabbage
Fresh fruit salad
Brownies

· CHRISTMAS ·

White Bean Dip with Fresh Ginger and Lime served with crackers
Cranberry Soup
Peppers Stuffed with Quinoa
Mexican Christmas Bread Pudding
Orange and Fennel Green Beans
Tossed salad
Fruit Compote with Cashew Cream

· KWANZAA ·

Kwanzaa Curried Rice Umoja or Fruits of the Harvest Pasta
Carrots in Love
Hoppin' John
Braised Collards with Ginger and Chili Pepper
Tossed salad with Sweet French Dressing
Whole wheat rolls
Carrot Cake

· NEW YEAR'S BUFFET ·

Garbanzo-Cashew Loaf (chilled and used as a spread on crackers)
Hoppin' John over rice
Oregon Tuscan Salad
Irish Soda Bread with Sun-Dried Tomatoes
Tossed salad of mixed greens
Gingerbread Cake with Lemon Hard Sauce

• EASTER •

Starving Artists' Banquet
Mama Bellini's Steamed Asparagus with Garlic and Lemon
Carrot and Raisin Salad
Irish Soda Bread with Aniseed and Raisins
Chocolate Cake with Raspberry Filling

• PASSOVER •

Vegetable Walnut Pâté with matzoh
Potato Vegetable Soup
Sweet and Sour Vegetables
Sweet Potatoes with Apples and Ginger
Beet Salad
Haroseth
Baked fruit

Recommended Cookbooks

· ESPECIALLY FOR BEGINNING VEGETARIAN COOKS ·

American Wholefoods Cuisine
by Nikki and David Goldbeck
New American Library, 1983

*The Complete Whole Grain
Cookbook*
by Carol Gelles
Donald Fine, 1989

The New Laurel's Kitchen
by Laurel Robertson, Carol
Flinders, and Brian Ruppenthal
Ten Speed Press, 1986

Simply Vegan
by Debra Wasserman and Reed
Mangels
The Vegetarian Resource Group,
1991

· FOR ALL VEGETARIAN COOKS ·

The Complete Vegetarian Cuisine
by Rose Elliot
Fodors Travel, 1990

Cooking Under Pressure
by Lorna Sass
William Morrow and Company,
1987

Flowers in the Kitchen
by Susan Belsinger
Interweave Press, 1991

Moosewood Cookbook
by Mollie Katzen
Ten Speed Press, 1992

Recipes from an Ecological Kitchen
by Lorna Sass
William Morrow and Company,
1992

*Great Vegetarian Cooking under
Pressure*
by Lorna Sass
William Morrow and Company,
1994

The Vegetarian Epicure
by Anna Thomas
Vintage, 1972

*World of the East: Vegetarian
Cooking*
by Madhur Jaffrey
Alfred A. Knopf, 1982

*The Vegetarian No-Cholesterol
Barbecue Cookbook*
by Kate Schumann and Virginia
Messina, M.P.H., R.D.
St. Martin's Press, 1994

*The Simple Soybean and Your
Health*
by Mark Messina, Ph.D., Virginia
Messina, R.D., and Kenneth D. R.
Setchell, Ph.D.
Avery, 1994

Index

♦